Sergeant Fricasse of the 127th Demi-Brigade

A REPRESENTATIVE OF THE PEOPLE WITH THE ARMY. (FIRST REPUBLIC.)

Sergeant Fricasse of the 127th Demi-Brigade

A French Soldier of the Revolutionary Period on Campaign, 1792-1802

ILLUSTRATED

Jacques Fricasse
Edited and Translated by John H. Lewis

LEONAUR

Sergeant Fricasse of the 127th Demi-Brigade
A French Soldier of the Revolutionary Period on Campaign, 1792-1802
by Jacques Fricasse
Edited and Translated by John H. Lewis

ILLUSTRATED

First published under the title
The Marching Journal of Sergeant Fricasse of the 127th Demi-Brigade 1792-1802

Leonaur is an imprint of Oakpast Ltd

Copyright in this form © 2022 Oakpast Ltd

ISBN: 978-1-915234-70-4 (hardcover)
ISBN: 978-1-915234-71-1 (softcover)

http://www.leonaur.com

Publisher's Notes

Contents

The Original Introduction Written in 1882

Fricasse! That famous stew of fried meat!

Comical is the name, but serious is the work, because it is defined by a rare sincerity. And genuine sincerity was most emblematic in this tormented period of the First Republic of France when every writer was passionate about taking sides for or against the new era. Enthusiastic praise or unworthy indictment, there was in those days hardly any middle ground.

This document, published here (in the original French) for the first time, at least has the merit of concerning no other war than that fought with foreign powers, no other enemies than those of the fatherland. It is authentic, and I personally hold at the disposal for the curious its original manuscript, which is of the time, and which was freely given to me by my friend, Jules de Forge de Vesoul. It is indeed a marching journal; each stage is noted there in its day, each fact of war appears at its proper time.

At a time when advancement was so rapid, there was no more humble career than that of our hero, and this is precisely what interested me in a work that does not offer, it must be said, literary seduction; it is as simple as the notebook of a citizen soldier who fulfilled his duty completely and modestly.

From 1792 to 1802, he campaigned every year: With the Army of Sambre-and-Meuse, he protected our holdings in the North and made his entry into Brussels. With the Army of the Rhine-and-Moselle, he pushed as far as Munich and accomplished the retreat which has become famous under the name of the 'Retreat of Moreau'. With the Army of Italy, he resisted in Genoa until the last extremity.

One of just nine survivors of a company of one hundred and ten men destroyed by the war, reduced by a wound to return to his village, he has neither a word of complaint, nor a tone of disappointed humour or ambition. He remains proud to have served his country with honour and probity. I insist on the use of this last word, because several pages of his diary bear witness to the noblest sentiments. The descriptive part is not very rich, the developments and the reflections are never pushed far, but if the spirit of the author is limited, his soul appears large and generous. One feels that he is an honest man and a good Frenchman. We overlook the dryness and the monotony of the story, because these surely makes one understand the spirit of the soldier and also the cruel necessities of the war he endured.

It is right that all know at what price one buys a victory.

Certainly, the courage to fire or to launch one's self into the enemy bayonets before you is already a great deal. But how many soldiers fell on the road before seeing a day of battle shine! How many obscure victims are devoted to endless marches, to the miseries of the bivouac, to the deprivation of comforts, to the sufferings of a winter campaign where rampant disease and hunger are unafraid of your gun.

One cannot imagine this by seeing a regiment marching past or reading an official report.

Other lessons emerge from our soldier's journal. It reveals the highest degree the expression of a republican faith which is not yet universally accepted without reservation. For the needs of certain causes, we have contradictorily exalted and belittled the volunteers of our own First Republic.

We will see that their moral strength was equal to their sufferings, if not their discipline. This is already an important point acquired in the debate which is not yet finished, but which, for the honour of our arms, does not lose value by being deepened. I see it without a spirit of exclusion, because I am one of those who see neither everything in pink, nor everything in black. It seems that the more we dig into the past, the less we become absolute. In history, the good and the bad remain as inseparable, in fact, as the shadow and light in a landscape. We only notice at certain times more light or more shade, and it is in the enhancement of this inequality that the truth of the painting is found.

If our volunteers of 1792 were not seasoned the first time they marched to war, they therefore really showed the national spirit, that is to say the will to ensure respect for France at the risk of their lives, which is the first quality of a soldier. We also note, and not without a certain surprise, that the sincere love of the Republic is imbued with a particular religious sentiment the expression of which is expressed at length in a prayer written at the end of its work. It has been collected with all the more care as it is a unique document of its kind. I had believed it at first copied from some text of the constitutional church, but its very incorrectness announces an original work; it is less surprising when we refer to the youth of the author who wrote it.

Le Journal de Fricasse has been published with all possible respect. I cut out repetitions and unnecessary words, spelling occasionally, but not allowing myself to add anything. (Restoring the spelling of the generally disfigured place names presented particular difficulties that I am not sure I always overcome. When in doubt, I used the question mark.)

To shed more light on the text, I have given a series of rigorously exact drawings of uniforms; they are placed at the end of this small volume with the necessary clarifications. From a military point of view, I did not have to concern myself with the discussion of facts, but what I have read of the reports of the time has proved to me that the author was telling the truth about the date and nature of the movements. The scope of them necessarily escapes him. We know that, except at the general staff, it is in the army that we are least informed about the general course of operations.

Precise as the data of our sergeant appears to be, a control text was nevertheless necessary and that was provided to us most relevantly by the *Memoirs* of a Marshal of the Empire who could not be suspected of inaccuracies. The young Soult was an officer in the same division as Fricasse; he supports the details given here by his own assertions, which we have frequently reproduced in the appropriate places. In this regard, we must pay tribute to the frankness with which the Duke of Dalmatia pays his tribute of admiration to the Republican Armies; he is honoured to have shared their poverty, their pride, their patriotic ardour. He declares that the fate of Poland was reserved for Republican France if the commitments made at Pilnitz could have been fulfilled.

He said:

But the French soldiers did not count the number of their enemies; they had faith in their own worth. Despite the setbacks they experienced at the beginning, the hardships they had to endure, the frequent replacement of their generals, the deep impression that the cries of the factions and the heartbreaks of the interior must have produced upon them, they always rose above them all. Of their fortune and their situation, they saw only duties to be fulfilled; and, drawing dangers upon themselves, they averted the eyes of the world from the scenes of desolation which covered the surface of France.

Then, speaking of the contrary fortune at the beginning of our arms, Soult adds:

The French paid for their tests by defeats and suffered the inevitable effects of the inexperience of their generals, the indiscipline of the troops, the vices of their organisation. The improvidence or greed of the administration, and the often-unfortunate influence of the representatives on the armies. It was a difficult time to go through, but when the army came out, it had re-immersed itself in it: the new leaders who were destined to secure victory, felt under the blow of these setbacks their intelligence developing, meditating on the faults they saw committing and formed in the middle of the ranks.

With regard to the changes undergone in the constitution of the army in 1794, Marshal Soult enters into no less endearing details about the spirit of our troops at the time; they cannot be deminished by being restated and can at any time provide a fine example

The officers set the example of dedication. The bag on the back, deprived of pay, (because it was only later, and when the assignats (paper money issued by the Constituent Assembly in France) had lost all their value, which they received in money, as well as the generals, eight *francs* a month), they took part in the distributions like the soldiers and received from the stores the clothing items that were essential to them. They were given a voucher to receive a coat or a pair of boots. However, no one dreamed of complaining of this distress, nor of looking away from the service which was the only study and the only subject of emulation. In all ranks, they showed the same zeal, the same eagerness to go beyond duty: if one stood out, the other sought to surpass him with his courage and his talents; this was the only way to proceed; mediocrity found nothing to be recommended. In the staffs, it was incessant work embracing all branches of the service, and yet it was not enough; we wanted to take part in everything that was being done. I can say it, it was the period of my career when I worked the most and when the chiefs seemed to me the most demanding. Also, although they did not all deserve to be taken as a model, many general officers, who later were able to surpass them, left their school. In the ranks of the soldiers, there was the same dedication, the same self-sacrifice. The conquerors of Holland crossed, in seventeen degrees of cold, the rivers and the inlets of the sea, and they were almost naked: however, they were in the richest country in Europe; they had all the seductions before their eyes, but discipline did not suffer the slightest attack. Never have the armies been more obedient, nor animated with more ardour: it is the epoch of wars when there was the most virtue among the troops. I have often seen the soldiers refuse before the fight the distributions that they were going to make to them and cry out: After the victory they will give them to us!

Our sergeant's diary bears the imprint of the enthusiasm to which a Marshal of the Empire wanted to pay homage. In this capacity alone, it deserves the confidence of the reader who seeks the truth in the facts; the incorrectness of their presentation does not detract from the greatness of the sentiment which dominates them. May our contemporaries condemn a love of well-being at all costs which threatens to distort our judgement of military duties! That a war occurs, it is only a concert of cries and lamentations in certain newspapers, if the food does not arrive at the appointed time and if the sick lack first aid. Very great misfortune, no doubt, but inevitable on campaign. However, it is who will analyse them in the most heart-breaking way to the cowardice of an entire nation. I read certain articles in 1871 about ambulance attendants which I could cite as models of this kind, primarily antinational sentiment

In peacetime, it manifests itself in another form. Mothers of volunteers write to newspapers to complain about the drudgery imposed on their sons; some volunteers themselves believe that they are heroes of self-sacrifice by publicising the story of their barracks' misfortunes. During the fall of 1881, did not a newspaper push the sensitivity to the point of being moved by the march of a regiment which had made, in the rain, from Lagny to Courbevoie!

Articles like this can be read at public meetings where desertion of the flag is proclaimed a social duty. In a more elevated class, I could cite more than one case of desertion abroad which was not withered as it should have been. In the middle of the living room, have I not heard a talented writer declare that the profession of arms was abject, and that the French would do much better to take an Army of Germans into their pay than to be stupidly killed by them!

Simple paradox, I will be told. But there are paradoxes as humiliating as confessions. In chauvinism, the childish exaggeration of patriotism has been ridiculed; let us fear the opposite ridicule which would be infinitely more dangerous. It is time to put your pride in knowing how to suffer. At that price alone, we can become as strong as our ancestors again.

The Journal of Sergeant Fricasse

I was born on the 13th of February 1773, in the village called
Autreville, two leagues from Chaumont en Bassigny, capital of the
Haute-Marne department. I am the legitimate son of Nicolas Fricasse,
gardener, and Anne Corniot, of the said parish. As soon as I was in the
world, my parents were called to be gardeners with the Lord of Juzen-
necourt. This is where I was brought up and where my parents taught
me what a decent man should know.

Then, my father went to cultivate the gardens of the Bernardins de
Clairvaux. This change has done a lot for my learning. My father was
one of the masters, and had four boys under his leadership. After three
years, he returned to take over his household, and I was given the same
job my father had. I will never forget a monk named Le Boulanger; he
was archivist and chief sacristan. This worthy man never ceased to give
me the opportunity to educate myself, but the idea was not foremost
in my mind, and I did not know how to take advantage of it.

He often said to me:

> Look at it this way, you can already read and write. Well! I want
> to teach you geography: it is very useful for a person who wants
> to take some trip.

In that time, I never thought I would leave him and I thought that
his great knowledge would serve me without learning. Ah!—how little I understood.

In those years, the States Generals met, and there was talk of the
abolition of convents. This changed many ideas, especially in the convent where I was, which consisted of ninety religious members. So,
they were abolished, and me too. I became a gardener with the Marquis de Messey, Lord of Beaux-le-Châtel. This lord gave me a lot of

praise; if he was happy. I was not so happy myself, for the land in his garden was too arid, and I had great difficulty in cultivating it.

As he was the first captain of a French cavalry regiment named the Royal-Étranger, stationed at Dôle in Franche-Comté, he left to join his regiment with all his family, and left us in the house with a coachman and a servant. I received a letter from him in which he told me to take care of his garden and his trees, and that on his return he would reward me. Present or absent, that did not prevent me from doing my service. Time went by without receiving his letters; I might as well have expected as much, for the marquis had emigrated with all his household he had at Dôle. So, I was resolved to leave him. We sold all the goods immediately after I left.

Leaving this house, I already knew where my place would be: I had been warned in advance by the new master and mistress. These kind people had come to see the garden, but I had only been able to promise them that I would join them at the proper time. So, I was now in the service of the citizen Quilliard, of Ville-sur-Laujeon—before the Revolution, Château-Villain. (The name of Château-Vilain has definitely survived.) They were virtuous people, hearts full of humanity; their good character was painted on their faces. All of this made me believe that I could spend happy days serving these generous citizens. After the work of the garden, came the hunting parties which the master of the house made almost every day with several citizens of the city. They were most often chasing large beasts including roe deer and wild boar, in the immense forests that the Duke of Penthièvre had in the neighbourhood.

I saw myself cherished by my masters, but I made sure to always remain so and to deserve their trust. Before long a battalion was required in the department. At that time Citizen Quilliard commanded the canton's national guard; he gave orders that all the communes assemble in the capital on August 24, 1792.

On the morning of the 24th, he told us:

> You probably know the job I have to do: we need several volunteers, those who want to leave my service are free. If, however, there are not enough volunteers, all the fathers and boys will be forced to draw lots. If it's not your plan to leave, well! my friends, I will do whatever is in my hands to be of service to you by sending others out for you.

So here we were in the city where all the township villages were gathered. In the first place, there were hardly any volunteers; it was one o'clock in the afternoon when several companies of the National Guard, composed of 160 men, had not yet been provided with the men they needed.

★★★★★★

In 1791, we had already formed National Guard battalions intended to join the army. Soult recalls, at the beginning of his *Memoirs*, that he was then in garrison in Schelestadt with the first battalion of Haut-Rhin. This body was numerous, he said, animated by a fine spirit, but very few of its officers were capable. One will find in no. 1 of our supplement an interesting extract of the *Memoirs* of Cagnot on the effects of the *levy en masse* which was then decreed.

★★★★★★

I had long been filled with desire for military service. How many times I had heard, through the papers, (public papers, newspapers), the news that our French Army had been pushed back and beaten everywhere! I was burning with impatience to see for myself things that it was impossible for me to believe. You will say that it was innocence that made me think thus, but I often said to myself: "Is it possible then that I only hear about misfortunes?" . . . Yes! it seemed to me that, if I had been present, the harm would not have been so great. I would not have said I was a better soldier than my compatriots, but I felt courage and I thought that, with courage, we overcome many things.

At this moment, to fulfil my duty, I presented myself at the head of the company; I asked them if they thought I was fit to join this battalion. Cries from all sides were heard: "Yes! we can't find a better one than you!"

So, I was recorded by the captain and the justice of the peace, without having informed my master of my feeling, when he offered to help me. I agree it wasn't done well on my part, but I was shy. Shyness and youth sometimes prevent one from expressing one's way of thinking.

It was eight days later, on August 24, that I left the house; I went to say goodbye to my father and my mother. It touched me very much to see the whole family shed tears over my departure without their consent. Since that moment, I began to travel. The reader will think whether I have done right or wrong in due course.

My battalion was required by General Biron; its title was *First battalion of Grenadiers and Chasseurs of Haute-Marne*.

The order for departure had finally arrived on September 2nd whereupon I went to Chaumont, capital of the department. We appointed provisional officers there who showed us the first principles of the school of the unarmed soldier. The names of these officers were: Ruel, captain, Barthelemy, lieutenant; Lemoine, sergeant-major; all three inhabitants of the city.

The order to form the battalion came, we left on October 5th for Saint-Dizier. On our way there, we stayed in Joinville; the stage was provided to us as well as the accommodation.

In Saint-Dizier, they made us take cantonments in the surroundings, while awaiting the organisation. I found myself in the part sent to Louvemont; in these cantonments, our route officers showed us the handling of weapons.

Left Louvemont on November 2nd, to return to Saint-Dizier, for our organisation. It was then that my companions honoured me with the rank of corporal in the sixth company; I had for captain, Lemoine; for lieutenant, Mongis; for second lieutenant, Thiébault.

After the battalion was organised, we were quartered again; but our new cantonments were three or four leagues farther from Saint-Dizier, where our staff has always remained. Two villages were intended for our company: Chamouilley, where the captain stayed with the first section, and Bienville where I was with the lieutenants: these villages are located on the Marne.

We did not make much of a living; a corporal was given twenty-three *sols* eight cents in paper a day (for some time it was six *sols* three *deniers* in silver, and eighteen *sols* in paper); a soldier had fifteen *sols* three *deniers* a day, all inclusive. With this pay, we were forced to buy everything we needed. Food was not expensive at that time; we could live reasonably.

We left these cantonments on January 21st to join the first section, and to prepare ourselves to celebrate the blessing of our flag, in Saint-Dizier.

One day after our arrival (the 24th), we assembled the battalion and we were taken to the local parish church. The blessing was made by our chaplain: afterwards, the whole battalion took the oath of fidelity in front of the flag. The flag had for an emblem a sword surmounted by a cap of freedom, and for the motto: *Eight hundred heads in a cap.*

At the same time, each company was given a pennant with its number on it. As the whole battalion could not stay in the city, because it was a crossing point, we were sent to resume our cantonments. The second section, of which I was a part, had difficulties with local ploughmen who did not want to rent us land for paper. To avoid any dispute, we were given another village called Narcy, half a league from the Marne. We spent the winter there.

Our staff changed to go to another town called Vassy. At this time, we changed cantonments. It was March 15th; we were in the outskirts of the city, we had for the company two villages which were called Brousseval and Domblain, where we received our complete clothing. Our battalion commander, named Deprée, often had the companies assembled to do manoeuvres. As we were in the Spring time, several times he made us get up at dawn, take up arms and put on our rucksacks; he took us two or three leagues to the military promenade. All this was done while waiting for the departure time.

I will not make great observations on the countryside where we stayed. It is a country where the world is very affable; it produces bread, wine and an infinity of other commodities; each individual lives there, content with his labour. We left these regions to go to Metz, on April 12th, by Bar-sur-Ornain, Saint Mihiel, Pont-à-Mousson.

Metz is a heavily fortified city of war, and, at that time, its fortifications were still being increased. We served in this place for three and a half months, and stayed in the Chambière quarters with the Swedish Regiment. We were trained to make the various fires. We left on August 17th from Metz for Maubeuge where part of the Army of the North was.

Before going any further, I will say that I had an illness in Metz that brought me to the brink of death. I attributed the cause of this disease to the air of the city, because I had always enjoyed the good country air. (The Chambière barracks have indeed always been considered unhealthy, because of the stagnant water from the pits which are in their vicinity.) Perhaps the distance of sixty leagues from the country also gave me these six weeks in hospital.

We will come back to our Northern Army. Here we were; it was soon that we would have to measure our weapons for the first time with those of our enemy. We could not stay in the camp because the tents were all full; we had to downgrade to the village of Beaufort, between Avesnes and Maubeuge (it was August 31st). There we found the Beaujolais Regiment.

There after it was bivouacs and early risings—night and day, because we were dealing with an enemy of which we were not the masters, and we were only very few people for the task.

September 7th—Left Beaufort for Ténières near the Sambre, where the enemy came to loot every day. We opposed their design. From there we went to Avesnes.

After a four hour rest, the *général* assembly was beaten. We left for Marbaix, on the road to Landrecies, where we bivouacked for forty-eight hours, following the movement of the enemy.

September 12th—At five o'clock in the morning, we arrived behind Landrecies. The head of the column began the attack behind the town, on the road to Quesnoy. We fired, but the enemy responded very well in the forest of Mormal where he was entrenched. However, their first entrenchments were removed, but the cutting of large trees prevented us from going any further. Our battalion entered the forest at eight in the morning. At seven in the evening, the column withdrew. We lost people in both parties. The enemy siege army came to give aid to the Observation Army. This is what made us retreat to the Landrecies glacis, otherwise they would have blocked us in the forest.

★★★★★★

The Army of the Prince of Cobourg had indeed occupied the Forest of Mormal by blocking Le Quesnoy. "Weak French detachments were watching his movements," said Soult; "they could not prevent it from deploying the immense means which had been prepared to reduce the place, it capitulated on September 11th, after having supported fifteen days of trenches. During the time that it succumbed, late efforts were made to free it: at Avesnes, by a division leaving Cambrai, at Fontaine, by another division leaving Landrecies: at the entrance to the forest of Mormal, by a column part of the Maubeuge camp." This last column is the one in question here.

★★★★★★

For our first battle, our success was not very great.

Three-hour rest on the Landrecies glacis; we were given some small refreshments. The column set off again; each corps was to resume its positions of September 7th.—A fifteen hour march. Our column, of twelve thousand men, both cavalry and artillery, had wanted to unblock Le Quesnoy and pass it through provisions. It was too late: when we arrived to attack the enemy observation army, the city surrendered; their last cannon shot was fired before the commencement of our attack.

Back in Beaufort, the bivouac began at one in the morning, half a league in front of the village, behind the Beaujolais Regiment which was encamped on a hill, a quarter of a league from the Sambre. The blockade of Maubeuge was expected day by day.

September 29th—We were bivouacking as usual, when an Austrian deserter came to the camp of Saint-Remi-Mal-Bâti; he said that the order was given in their regiment to be ready to cross the Sambre for four in the morning. The 68th Beauce Regiment was at this camp; it redoubled its duty and put itself on its guard. It was a very dark fog: so, the enemy took the opportunity to throw over their pontoons during the night, and, at four o'clock precisely, thirty thousand men passed, well assured of victory.

(*The details of the text are confirmed by a new passage from Soult's Memoirs; the slight difference given in the evaluation of the troops is more than cancelled out by the reinforcement which then arrives at the enemy.*)

The troops encamped on the heights near the Sambre made vigorous resistance, but could not hold out against such a large column, and were obliged to fall back on us, who were in the second line. We were unable to stop the march of the Austrians who were attacking us from all sides.

Retreated to the town of Maubeuge. In spite of our vigorous resistance, it was not long before we were blocked by their numerous cavalry which sought to seize the villages and the woods where we had to pass. As our skirmishers did not give them enough occupation and did not give us time to parade, we were forced to line up in front of the Beaufort Forest. As the enemy approached, we fired in line for three quarters of an hour. His artillery forced us to retreat a second time, after losing a cannon and several gunners killed and wounded. Twenty men of our battalion were put out of action. Our road was cut off; all that remained for our retreat was to go deep into the woods and get out again as best we could.

So, there we were. After having made half a league in this forest, being ready to go out, an enemy regiment which was hiding from our sight forced us to seek another passage. On another edge of the woods, the enemy surrounded us in the same way. My faith! there was no room to swing a cat. Being taken prisoner did not accommodate us; we broke through the enemy who did not cease to continually shoot at us.

From this forest, we joined the column that was gathering in the plain, on the side of the road to Frieville. We still wanted to resist the foe, but in vain. We had to take shelter in the camp and arrange the redoubt artillery to defend the approaches. The enemy seized the villages around the city and looted our belongings that were left there.

Thirty men of our battalion, who remained in the Beaufort Forest without having been able to break through to join us, had been forced to retreat into the woods. Along the way, they captured an Austrian sentry. This soldier, very happy to be a prisoner, helped our men out of the woods and led them to a place, which was the least guarded, where they were able to pass between the posts unseen since it was a dark night (30th September). These soldiers went to do service in Avesnes, and joined us after the release of Maubeuge.

That same night, around ten o'clock in the evening, our battalion took charge of the Wolf Redoubt for twenty-four hours. After being relieved, we went to take a position to the left of the entrenched camp of Falise; that was the name of the Maubeuge camp.

Day by day we waited for the siege, but in vain. It has been reported by several people that General Cobourg's intention was not to besiege the city, but to make it surrender by famine, because it was not provided with any food. There were twenty thousand men able to bear arms, both in the camp and in the town; at the time of the blockade, we took an oath to die with weapons in hand rather than surrender to the orders of a tyrant.

October 6th—Attacked with six thousand men, but without success. They showed up triple and double what we were. We only got away with a great loss.

October 7th—Same failure. We are invested from all sides without being able to give ourselves enlargement.

On October 5th, at the left redoubt, between the Bois du Tilleul and our outposts, a French sentry and a Dutch sentry were sixty paces from each other, which made it easy for them to converse. Four soldiers from my post came forward; the Dutch, who were in the Bois du Tilleul, were drawn by curiosity to join in the conversation. However, a Frenchman recognised his brother among the Dutch, who was the most eager to ask how we were, what we thought, and if we did not lack food.

Answer: "The Republicans are not missing anything."

In derision, they replied that we were already eating our horses, and that, with our paper, our assignats, we had to starve. They added that they kept us in their nets, that they would make us dance the *carmagnole (a lively street dance and song popular with the first radical French republicans)* one last time. This one said that, although French, he would

20

take pleasure in seeing us tear our tongues out.

A volunteer said to him: "Comrade, you do not appear to be Dutch, and no doubt it has not been long since you left France. You seem very bloodthirsty for a country which contains your parents, but which you must not hope to see again, because the law pronouncing your death sentence would make your head fall. This is what is reserved for rascals of your kind."

His brother, who had recognised him, interrupted the conversation by saying: "Let me see this rascal! He used to be my brother."

The other says: "If I was your brother, I still am."

The volunteer said no, that he had made himself unworthy of it. "You know, unhappy man," he added, "that I left voluntarily. May he remember the promise made! You promised to take care of our mother, but you twisted your oath, you left her without sustenance and in grief; you are unworthy of living, you are not a human, but a true barbarian."

(Note that this generous soldier shared half of his pay with his mother.)

The Dutch, who understood a little French, did not fail to blame him, and the coward withdrew. His brother cocked his rifle, shot and struck him in the thigh. He got up and plunged into the wood.

An Austrian dragoon, of the Regiment of Coburg, charged one of ours, of the 12th Dragoons. After each firing their pistol, they approach to cut each other. What a surprise! They recognise each other as brothers; for fifteen years they had not seen each other. Instantly, their sabres drop, they leaped from their horses and throw themselves at each other's necks, unable to say a single word. A moment later, they swore not to separate and live under the same banner. Our dragoon went to find General Jourdan to beg him not to regard his brother as a deserter or as a prisoner, and the general consented to incorporate this man into the regiment.

Happy time of October 18th! It's to a column of eighty thousand men, commanded in chief by General Jourdan, that we owe our freedom.

★★★★★★

Jourdan's army actually numbered only 45,000 combatants; they did not come from Vendée, but from the camps of the Army of the North and the Army of the Ardennes. We will find in number 2 of our supplement a moving account of the combat which brought about the lifting of the blockade of Maubeuge; it is taken from the *Mémoires de*

Carnot, by his son. (Paris, Pagnerre, 1862. Volume 1). The remarkable details found there formed a necessary complement to our text.

★★★★★★

They fought, for two days, with fearlessness. This combat was initiated by a number of skirmishers with artillery; the cavalry and the rest of the infantry then supported. On the third day, the fog was less thick; the light gave strength to our weapons, and, despite their strong fears, our army routed them.

These eighty thousand men came from Vendée, were commanded by a republican; but also, the troops assisted him. They made the Austrian Army cross the Sambre again, which took advantage of the night to disappear, leaving a quantity of tools used for the work of their redoubts.

I will report here what the Austrian soldiers told us: "Hey! Little *carmagnole*, (once again allusion to the famous revolutionary round called: *carmagnole*), you will not get out of here unless you are in our power. Our general said that if your red bonnet was of the strength to make the imperial eagle leave, and raise the siege, he would adopt your constitution and be of the party of the republicans. (The remark was indeed attributed to the Prince of Cobourg, who then commanded the besieging army.) He did not adopt it, but he had the Republicans *chase* him

October 18th—Leaving our camp to explore, we went to Hautmont, a village to the left of Maubeuge, all in disarray. It was after the harvest; the enemy used the grain to make barracks and feed the horses. It was the greatest desolation. The homes of farmers devastated and even largely burnt down. See what war is. Woe to the country where it is takes place! The inhabitants there can only be unhappy.

Although we were not long blocked, I would say that we already felt our misery, food was cut off from us (rationed); the river passed below our camp, but the enemy had cut off the water; we were obliged to take it from the ditches of the entrenchments where we were going to take care of the necessities. The rain, which continually fell, made it all mix together. So many of us had suffered with the bloody flux there.

The enemy had been pushed back, but we must keep his passages covered.

October 29th—Left Hautmont to go to the right of Maubeuge, in a village called Marpent, on the banks of the Sambre, where from time to time we wished each other, 'Good Morning' with rifle shots with the Austrian posts.

November 14th—Left Marpent to go to the Saint-Remy camp, on the heights, until the 29th. This last day, we went to Colleret.

RECOLLECTIONS OF THE YEAR, 1794

We left Colleret for Damousies on January 12th, 1794, the second year of the Republic. All these villages were in the front line, near to the enemy outposts; for the Imperialists had a passage over the Sambre, near Beaumont, so that we were obliged to guard ourselves everywhere. They were going to forage for the cavalry on their borders, because forage was not very abundant in countries where the troops are still encamped.

From Damousies, we came on January 19th to the village of Aibes, still on the front line where the bivouac was continuous. There, I passed sergeant, by seniority of rank, on 26th P*luviôse (5th month of the Republican calendar-approximately mid-January to mid-February)*.

During this time, we received recruits from the requisition, and the companies were fully manned. We hardly had time to show all these men the first principles of exercise than that we had to go and fight; also, the harshness of winter caused us many troubles. In those days, there was no armistice: winter and summer, we were always on campaign in the countryside.

Left Aibes on 6 *Germinal (7th month of the Republican calendar, approximately mid-March to mid-April)* to go to Jeumont. Half the battalion has encamped half a league to the right, at a wood called Bois de l'Abbaye Brulee. Every four days, the posts were raised forty feet from the enemy, and in other places there was only the Sambre that separated us. In this place, many times we said good morning to each other with gunshots. All both sides wanted was to surprise each other at the posts and remove the sentries.

On the 22nd, we started from this position. The enemy made new attempts to block Maubeuge. Another half hour later, it was done. But the brave Army of the North was not discouraged. We retreated two leagues near Cerfontaine, where the headquarters was situated. The whole troop was in a line, ready for the fight, which immediately began. The Austrian column was pushed back beyond its positions, leaving a very large number of dead, wounded and prisoners.

We resumed our position in the village. We found there some of their foot *chasseurs* who had crossed the Sambre to plunder; we took

Imp. de Galban.

Chasseur volontaire. — **Officier porte-drapeau.**

Infanterie de ligne.

1794.

them prisoners, and the rest of the day was spent giving each other 'Republican Salutes'. (Exchanging gunshots.)

Before leaving the borders of Hainaut, for the other bank of the Sambre, I will talk about the situation of the inhabitants. Most no longer had homes (and still many more had lost their lives!) I compare the enemy at this time to a hail that leaves nothing in the countryside over which it passes.

In these fertile regions, these inhabitants lived in peace; their lands produced good wheat, all kinds of grains, fruits and vegetables. Wine, being very expensive, was not much in use; beer was the drink for ordinary folk. Their way of life was very simple: milk, cheese and fruit, this was their diet. Very beautiful horned cattle were kept; each inhabitant has more or less prosperity according to the size of his pasture; these had enclosures surrounded by woods of all kinds from which they drew heating for the winter; in these enclosures, they cut the first hay; after that, their cows remained there until winter without returning to the byre. You hardly see the villages until you are inside them; they are all enclosed, with large woods all around and near to each house. Most of the houses are covered with straw in this country.

8th Floréal.—We entered the town of Beaumont after a battle with the Emigrants (*Émigrés*) where there were many who remained dead on the field. We took very few prisoners because they did not willingly surrender. We have driven the enemy from their strong positions around the city; we got hold of it on the spot; they were to our advantage.

18th—Arrived at Beaumont camp. Left on the 20th at eight o'clock in the evening, crossing the city to bivouac, until daybreak, on the road to Mons, two leagues ahead. At daybreak, we advanced on the enemy encamped in the plain. His arrangements for receiving us were not prompt enough; he fled from our first attack. In this same affair, I was detached with sharpshooters to flush out their marksmen from a village; we took eight and killed a few. The rest fled.

22nd—After making several movements, despite the rain that fell every day and made the roads impassable, we stopped in the plain of Beaumont to spend the night there.

23rd—At daybreak, the troop was divided into three columns; those on the right and on the left attacked the enemy with so much ardour that they made them throw themselves at us in the centre. For more than half an hour we had heard the cannon roaring and the muskets shooting. There was a discontented murmur in our column that we were inactive. Suddenly, we saw the enemy manoeuvring upon us, they were not received with less daring by us than our comrades. We forced them to retreat to the Sambre; several of them drank more of its waters than they wanted to. We went after them; we pushed them more than two leagues at the charge. We took several cannons, many prisoners; a very large number of them were killed. We would not have stopped pursuing them if the night had not prevented us from continuing.

24th—We set off again at daybreak. A column ran along the Sambre; the other was advancing to the right. The enemy awaited us in their strong redoubts. We did not hesitate. The fire started with a very lively cannonade. Our artillery began to respond with ardour, it was supported by the fire of the infantry who advanced at a charge and took the redoubt by force, despite a terrible enemy fire. The troops displayed a courage worthy of true Republicans.

We took four cannons and their caissons from them, several prisoners and many of them were killed. We pursued them, 'bayonet to the kidneys', for half an hour, they reached a village behind which they took position, with a reinforcement that came to them from the Grisvel camp under Maubeuge, which held us in check in front of the village called Grand-Reng. We got in line in front of the village and we sent a large number of skirmishers who at first captured the village; it was taken back from them: they returned, but coming on board from the other side, pieces of grape-shot developed their fire on them, it was impossible to override. For eight hours, the fire did not stop from one side to the other. In the evening, our ammunition ran out, we were obliged to give up our position to them and to retake the Sambre. We had lost more than enough people in the struggle.

★★★★★★

Marshal Soult gives the following details about the Grandreng fight. "The failure experienced by the centre column rendered the movement of General Mayer on Haulchin useless, and allowed the Prince of Kaunitz to march in support of his right, to Grandreng, by stripping his left. General Dejardins had already removed some redoubts, and he was entering the village, when all of a sudden, his two divisions were themselves assailed and overwhelmed by the Austrian cavalry. They made, with the support of the Duhesme brigade, a last effort to return to Grandreng; but they failed again and were obliged to hasten their retreat to retake the Sambre, despite the support they received from the cavalry reserve. The Austrian general acquired the honour of this day by making his forces mobile, from left to centre, and from centre to right, where he successively took the superiority. Its losses were much less than those of the French, who sacrificed more than four thousand men and twelve pieces of cannon."

★★★★★★

The previous days had been favourable. That day, we lost almost all the ground we gained, but we still had our passage on the Sambre. So, the work to start over again. Let us see if we do it the in same way. We had to walk all night to get to the plain, where we had been on the 22nd.

25th—Despite the continuous rain and bad weather, we changed our position as we approached the enemy. We had only the sky for cover.

26th—We came forward to oppose the march of the Austrian Army on the banks of the Sambre. The combat began with our *tirailleurs* drawn from the companies in turn; the artillery supported them from morning to night with success; it defeated cavalry platoons, dismantled several pieces; our shells blew up caissons, killed many soldiers and horses. Some of our soldiers were shouting: "Come, soldiers of the imperial eagle, you will not long resist the ardour of the *sansculottes* soldiers!"

Our loss was not great that day; a cannon ball killed two horses. We spent the night under arms.

27th—Took position in the village of Hantes, on the Sambre. The enemy made an attempt to pass through where we were, but they did not succeed.

30th—Left our position to go to the heights of Lobbes Abbey. This abbey was burnt down when the Austrians retired.

1st Prairial—We are going to attack the enemy; artillery and skirmishers begin. Sustained shooting from noon to night. On the 2nd, the fight began in the same way, but with much more success; the enemy retreated to his strong redoubts near Grand-Reng, where the fire lasted until evening. Bloody day for both parties; we retired to the heights near Grand-Reng. The posts were established very close to those of the enemy. We stayed a few days in this position.

★★★★★★

Sans Culottes

"The setbacks of the 13th had irritated the representatives without enlightening them; they will order a new passage, but the operations, even more badly directed than the first time, resulted in much greater losses." (Soult.)

★★★★★★

5th—We transferred our column of cavalry and part of the infantry to make them pass to the right which was not strong enough. The enemy saw this movement and prepared to fight.

We had no orders to take up arms in the morning. Usually, it is in the morning that the big hits are made. We were quiet under the little windbreaks we had made with tree branches; a very thick fog prevented our outposts from discovering the movements of the enemy when he surprised them. Immediately one heard shouting from all sides: To arms! Everyone ran to line up. They were already in our camp, and their cavalry was advancing with great strides on the road to Mons. There was a twelve-piece cannon and an eight-piece cannon loaded with grape; our gunners immediately set fire to it and delayed their march. They were much stronger than us; nevertheless, they were received in a republican manner, but, in spite of our vigorous resistance, we were obliged to retreat and to retake the Sambre. In our column, there was only the No. 22 Cavalry Regiment at the time of the retreat. We had a hundred men out of action. The rest of the day was spent tugging. Spent the night in Jeumont; the bridge which served us is called Solre-sur-Sambre

On the 5th *Prairial* affair, near Grand-Reng, Citizen Mercier, a rifleman of Horiot's company (3rd battalion), native of Provenchères, district of Joinville (Haute-Marne), fought an Austrian hussar. Two sabre cuts to the head and to the left wrist overwhelmed him.

"Surrender, rascal!" said the hussar.

"A coward would," said Mercier. "But not me!"

He got up, took his rifle in his right hand, put the barrel on the bleeding left arm, put his finger on the trigger and killed the hussar. But the injuries of this true republican were very severe. He died a month later.

In this affair I saw brave republicans covered with wounds gathering all their strength just as they were about to breathe their last breath, rushing forward to kiss the cockade, the sacred pledge of our conquered freedom; I heard them send ardent wishes to heaven for the triumph of the armies of the republic.

Cailac, one of our captains, had his leg shattered by a cannon ball,

29

and was dead three weeks afterwards, saying: "My life is nothing; I would give it a thousand times for the republic to triumph." Hit in the stomach by shrapnel, a battalion grenadier said to those who wanted to help him: "Leave me, my friends, let me die! I'm happy, I served my homeland." And he then expired.

7th—At daybreak, we set off and we went to the village of Hantes. As our provisions were delayed, we began to thresh wheat, go to the mill and we baked our own bread. I will say that all the inhabitants of these villages had withdrawn into the woods, because the armies caused them too much harm. It seems that heaven wants to increase ours; rain is our share every day.

8th—Left Hantes to go and camp on the heights of the Aune abbey.

12th—Left our positions at eight o'clock in the evening to go to the Aune abbey, we arrived there at midnight, the same day. This abbey was completely devastated and burnt.

14th—We passed the Sambre, which is very close to there.

15th—The troops set off and we attacked at daybreak. Combat was initiated by a strong cannonade. The enemy abandoned his positions; we seized the heights.

16th—The cannonade was heard from the Army of the Ardennes, which is under the walls of Charleroi. The enemy moved there in force, with a reinforcement of fifty thousand men, and the so-called Emperor at their head. That day, they relieved the city, pushed us back to the edge of the Sambre near the Aune abbey where we are staying for three days.

19th—We left for Hantes, where we arrive at eleven o'clock in the evening, very tired of continual walking.

★★★★★★

Marshal Soult said here: "We must also admire the docility of the troops, whom no setback could destroy, and deplore the fact that, subject to the tyrannical authority of the representatives, they did not have at their head leaders worthy of them. For the past fortnight, the corps which were on the Sambre had lost more than fifteen thousand men and half of their material; the soldiers lacked food and were in dire need of rest. The generals made the request to Saint-Just; In the council, Kleber observed that they were going to see the arrival, before ten days, of the Army of the Moselle, of which we will speak shortly, and that one had only to wait for it, while occupying itself to repair the losses of the army, to resume operations with all the more vigour. But *Tomorrow we need a victory for the Republic. Choose between a siege or a battle.* We had to choose, we marched on May 26 on Charleroi.

"Despite the success he had just achieved, the Prince of Kaunitz had been replaced by the Prince of Orange in command. The allied troops were on the Sambre, to defend its passage; they also occupied, above Marchiennes-au-Pont, the entrenched camp of the Tomb, which covered Charleroi. Kléber and Marceau were in charge of attacking it, and General Fromentin to carry off the bridge of Lernes. These two attacks failed by the excessive fatigue of the troops, who showed hesitation and remained exposed to the strongest fire, rather than advancing. At nightfall, however, the enemies evacuated the camp, leaving only a fortified post in Marchiennes." (Soult.)

This last paragraph explains how our sergeant will speak of retirement after having spoken of a victory which was undoubtedly a partial advantage without result on the whole of the day.

★★★★★★

21st—Arrived at six o'clock in the morning at Thuin, a town from which the enemy had been driven out a few days before.

22nd—Left at one in the morning for Baudribut camp.

24th—At daybreak, we passed the Sambre and camped in front of the town of Fontaine l'Évêque.

28th—Raising of the camp. We attacked at one in the morning to promote the siege of Charleroi. The attack was lively and started with the fire of the skirmishers. Their cavalry, which saw only skirmishers, charged on them; this fog prevented them from seeing the battalions which were lying in ambush behind the hedges. When they saw that the cavalry was half a gun range, they fired in line. Several killed, a few prisoners; the rest fled. We followed, we met their infantry who could not resist our ardour, we took many prisoners, we took two pieces of cannon with their caissons fully harnessed.—After this conquest, we returned to our position near Fontaine l'Evêque; having arrived, we were ordered to go to Baudribut camp where the park was; arrived at the entrance of the night, we stayed there a few days.

30th—We broke camp at two in the morning and passed the Sambre for the last time at four. We came to stand to the left of Fontaine l'Évêque. At noon, the enemy advanced on two of our companies

31

which were in front; he wanted to surprise them. Our battalions, who saw the manoeuvre, got into line and stood ready to march, when a scout came to tell us that they were retreating. We immediately set off to pursue them; their rear-guard cavalry wanted to charge us, to delay our march, but it was received in a republican manner, a discharge very quickly made them share the retreat.

2nd Messidor—We followed the enemy without finding resistance; they left us several pieces of cannons and caissons fully harnessed. Our cavalry took a large number of prisoners of the Austrian infantry. The night suspended the victory, but it prepared a new one by letting us make risers in favour of its darkness to prepare for the fight at the break of day.

7th—The enemy has shown itself in force to unblock Charleroi, but we have stood in the way of its plan.

The fire started at four in the morning and lasted part of the day. Night spent under arms to the left of the Trazegnies camp. Left this camp at three in the morning to go and meet with the Moselle Army. While walking, we were made to stay in a covered path, in front of a village, not far from Charleroi. It is in this place that we learned of the surrender of the place (of 7th *Messidor*, at eleven o'clock in the morning) with fifty thousand men, eighty guns and several small stores.

★★★★★★

A singularly exaggerated figure. Soult reports a sad episode of the siege: "Colonel Marescot directed the operations of the engineers, under the eyes of Generals Jourdan and Hatry; we had a sufficient artillery crew and representatives Saint-Just and Lebas stood at the foot of the trenches to hasten the work. One day, they were visiting the site of a battery that had just been traced: 'At what time will it be over?' Saint-Just asked the captain in charge of having it executed. 'It depends on the number of workers I will be given, but we will work tirelessly on it,' replied the officer. 'If tomorrow at six is not in a condition to fire, your head will fall!' . . . . In this short delay, it was impossible for the work to be finished; however, as many men as the space could contain some.

"It was not entirely finished when the fatal hour struck. Saint-Just kept his horrible promise: the artillery captain was immediately arrested and sent to his death, for the scaffold marched after the fierce representatives. If we hadn't been victorious, most of our leaders would have suffered the same fate. We learned later that Saint-Just had placed several army generals on a proscription list, and that he under-

32

stood me therein, although I was only a colonel. Jourdan was to be sacrificed first; he had replaced Hoche in the command, and he had, like him, incurred the hatred of the representative by the courageous resistance he offered to his wishes, when the presumptuous ignorance of Saint-Just claimed to direct military operations." (Soult.)

★★★★★★

Out on the same day, the garrison laid down their weapons in front of us; it was immediately escorted and taken to France. This city was bombed without our doing much entrenchment, because it was unlocked several times.

8th—We went out of our covered way to oppose the parade of Austrian columns sent to surround us. That day they had joined forces on both sides to give us a *hunt*, and raise the siege of Charleroi which had been delivered; but they were not informed of it, for they had thrown out their plan so well that they sought to catch us in the crossfire. There was no room to swing; the combat began at eight o'clock in the morning with a strong cannonade, from all sides, with unequalled rapidity, as never before had been heard.

Our courage already seemed to announce victory to us, alas hand of fate! in a fire so terrible and so obstinate, ammunition ran out. We therefore had to retreat and withdraw faster than we would have liked, encountering obstacles, ditches, a village whose streets were so narrow that the troops did not know where to pass and saw themselves almost in the power of the enemy.

The Austrian columns advanced quickly to take us in flank. But we got to the top of the mountain earlier than they did, and we used up what little ammunition we had left. We delayed their march. I will say that as we ascended this mountain, cannonballs and shells and bullets fell among us like hail, but it had very little effect, although they were very close to us. We lost very few people and, thanks to the surrender of Charleroi, we retreated under its glacis. He only retired with pain and loss.

★★★★★★

Marshal Soult thus completes the story of this day. "It was seven in the evening. For some moments the fight had ceased at the wings; it was allowed to finish in the centre without pursuing the enemies. Exhausted with fatigue and want, the soldiers could barely stand, and they also lacked ammunition. There was no possibility of continuing the pursuit, some advantages which could have been obtained; officers and soldiers, all cried out: 'A golden bridge to the departing enemy!' and the troops were given an indispensable rest.

"The next day there was no movement; it was necessary to recover from such a day and pick up the debris which covered the battlefield. The losses were counted; our number amounted to nearly five thousand *hors de combat*, and by the number of the dead, those of the enemy were estimated at more than seven thousand men; on both sides there were only a few prisoners. Among those we did, there were Frenchmen, part of the Royal-German regiment and that of Berching-hussar, to whom the law passed against *émigrés* taken with arms in hand was applicable. Not a soldier thought that it was possible to deliver to the scaffold those we had just fought face to face.

"During the night, we made it easier for them to escape, limiting ourselves to telling them that elsewhere they would atone for the error of having armed themselves against their country; several later returned to join our ranks. In the course of the war, we saved a large number of French people who were in the same situation, and they received protection and advancement among us; many of them thus obtained to be eliminated from the fatal list and to return to their confiscated property. We have to believe that they have retained some recognition."

★★★★★★

During the siege of Charleroi, a gunner from the Swedish regiment cried out as he died: "Cobourg, Cobourg, with your many florins, you will not have paid a drop of my blood; I pay it all today for the Republic and for freedom."

All those who lost their lives in this siege, in the midst of the most acute pains, gave no sign of complaint. Their faces were calm and serene; their last word was: Long live the Republic! It is in the bed of honour that we must see our warriors, to learn the difference that exists between free men and slaves. The servants of kings expire cursing the cruel ambition of their masters. The defender of liberty blesses the blow that struck him; he knows that his blood only flows for freedom, glory and for the support of his country.

In the left column and that on the right, which was the Army of the Moselle, the cannon did not stop roaring all day. The fight was bloody like it never seemed before.

★★★★★★

This is well confirmed by Marshal Soult's account: "In our ranks, enthusiasm grew with the danger; Since the beginning of the action, and throughout its duration, the rallying cry of the *avant-garde* has always been: 'No retreat today, no retreat!' So, everything that came up against her was shattered. Surrounded by bloody debris, its camp in flames,

34

most of its cannons dismantled, its caissons exploding at any moment, heaps of corpses filling in the entrenchments, the most vivid attacks constantly renewed, nothing was capable of intimidating it, not even the burning of the countryside that surrounded us on all sides. The fields, covered with ripe wheat, had been set alight by our fire and that of the enemy; no one knew where to stand to avoid it; but we were determined to only emerge victorious from this volcano."

The courage of the leaders had, on more than one point, only been able to maintain the troops, as this other passage clearly shows:

"Before six o'clock in the morning, the allies had made progress, and the divisions of the Ardennes repassed the Sambre, in complete disorder, at the bridges of Tamine and Ternier, leaving their general to guard alone, with his officers and some orders, the position that they had just left. I had been sent by General Lefebvre, to ascertain the state of our right, and to provide for the arrangements which circumstances required. I joined Marceau between the woods of Lépinoy and the hamlet of Boulet, just as the enemies were about to surround him. He challenged them, and in his despair, he wanted to be killed, to erase the shame of his troops.

"I stopped him: 'You want to die,' I said to him, 'and your soldiers dishonour themselves: go find them and come back to win with them!' Waiting, we will keep the position to the right of Lambusart.— 'Yes, I hear you,' cried Marceau, 'it is the road to honour! I run there; before long I will be at your side.' Two hours later, he had brought back the bravest, and he took part in our success."—These extracts give an idea of the phraseology of the time; we gladly used the big words that we laugh at today, but the acts were also big, which scoffers should not forget either.

★★★★★★

Twice the right column has been repulsed, and twice it has won the victory; it took fifteen pieces of cannon of all calibre from them. The left column had the same success. Sometimes, whoever thinks he wins is overcome; with their great strength they tried to block us, and they were taken anyway.

We have lost a few brave republicans, but we can judge the loss of the enemy, always great for those who are forced to flee. This day was one of the victorious days of the Republic, it will forever bear the name of the *Battle of Fleurus*.

On this memorable day of 8 *Messidor*, an unfortunate woman forsaken by her husband who had emigrated and had nothing to live on was, in man's clothes, with her brother, in her company rank. The company being dispersed in skirmishers, the enemy skirmishers, who

35

BATTLE OF FLEURUS, 26TH JUNE, 1794

had had a little advantage for a while, came to charge ours in the *mêlée*; it found itself with few people surrounded by a large number of Austrians. She got away with blowing the brains out of whoever held her, never ceasing to say that she would never surrender, that her life was sacrificed for her homeland. These tyrants promised to respect her sex and to take her only as a prisoner. This woman was, with her brother, in the 22nd Cavalry Regiment, which today repaired the mistake it had made near Grand-Reng.

Before the capture of Charleroi, while we were bivouacking on the heights of Fontaine-l'Évêque, the enemy, not believing themselves in strength, contented themselves with sending us cannon-balls and shells. We lost several men, including a battalion drummer. A shrapnel pierced his skin sac and his side; he remained dead in the square; two other soldiers were wounded at the same time. A Chamborant hussar passing through the square, took the drum and got behind an oak, beating the charge with the handle of his knife, which put the enemy to flight.

9th—We have come to take the positions we had previously.

12th—We walked all day to bivouac in front of the town of Binche. Arrived at eleven o'clock in the evening, we spent the rest of the night under arms. The attack began with a heavy cannonade.

15th—We left to attack the retreating enemy towards Mons. At eight o'clock in the morning, our sharpshooters advanced at a charge with two guns, they pursued the Austrians so strongly that they did not have time to enter the city of Mons. Our cavalry seized the passages in the outskirts of the city and immediately battalions entered, bayonets in front. In that day about two hundred prisoners were made. The other columns continued for two more hours. The night has stretched its veils, (*this poetic image would be surprising if we did not refer to the popular songs of the past where mythology still played a big role*); we had to stop our march. We spent the night under the walls of Mons.

16th—The city returned, we went to take position in front of the village named Beausoir.

17th—Left this position at daybreak, thinking to find the Austrians, but we travelled five leagues without meeting anyone.

Camped in front of Braine-le-Comte, located on the road from Mons to Brussels. We entered the city with the liveliest applause of all the *bourgeoisie* who shouted: "*Long live the French Republican soldiers!*"

21st—We broke camp to continue our journey. We entered the town of Hal with the same applause; we camped in front of the city until the 23rd. We left at daybreak, believing to find those who threatened us a few days before. Our vanguard was enough to make them disappear.

23rd—We entered the city of Brussels, likewise with the loudest applause of all the *bourgeoisie*: "Long live the republican soldiers!" As we were at the head of the column, we stayed in place, under arms, while the column marched. It went on all through the night.

24th—The rest of the column has passed. Immediately, the troops were brought into the barracks, but half of them were still under arms. Our battalion was in the Old Market district; and the other two battalions were in big *bourgeois* houses. We had the Swedish regiment and the Haut-Rhin battalion with us. We were without any supplies. (*Barracks supplies.*)

30th—We left at one in the morning. We went to camp in front of Louvain. I had left three days earlier with a picket of twenty-five men to escort the boats that we had picked up in Villebruck, on the canal that comes to Brussels. We were well received in this place which is five leagues away. We arrived on the 30th with these boats loaded with hay and oats for the stores in Brussels, and I joined, with my picket, the demi-brigade which was encamped in front of the town of Louvain.

1 Thermidor—Left at daybreak, we came to stand before the town of Tienen, where we found our enemy, we attacked him without further ado and pursued him two leagues. We have returned to our position.

7th—Having left at daylight, we went to stand in front of the town of Saint-Tron.

9th—We made a move, we went to camp in a large plain close enough to Tienen, where we heard the cannon of our vanguard roaring, which did not give the Austrian Army time to rally.

16th—Leaving this camp, we came to the Berlingen camp.

29th—We made a movement of a quarter of a league at the entrance of the night. We passed through a village that separated our camp from Looz camp. All these plains where we were encamped were entrenched on the enemy's side by strong redoubts.

The Army of Sambre and Meuse.

1st Fructidor—It is in this camp that we were amalgamated with the regiment of Beauce and a battalion of Haut-Rhin.

★★★★★★

We were moving forward with the enrolment. This important operation was carried out with the greatest rigidity; the generals had to choose, under their responsibility, among the battalion chiefs, the most capable to designate them as brigade chiefs. The instructions of the representatives of the people read: "Ranks are not the property of individuals; they belong to the Republic, which has the right to dispose of them only in favour of those who are in a position to render it services." Three times stronger than before their meeting, the new bodies exhibited more regularity as a whole and more self-confidence.

★★★★★★

The officers and non-commissioned officers assembled; we celebrated for two days, we drank the wine of the alliance, we swore to ourselves that brotherhood would reign between us until death; and as we served the same country, we promised ourselves to always live in peace as brothers and true supporters of the French Republic. The number that this demi-brigade had at that moment was 127; it was first commanded by Brigadier General Richard and General of Division Poncet.

In this camp, we learned of the surrender of Valenciennes. 227 guns and quantity of powder and other well-stocked magazines were found in this place, more than had been found when they were delivered.

14th Fructidor—We left at two o'clock in the morning: we were encamped in the plain of Maestricht, and we were still three leagues away in the second line. The straw was delivered to the whole column.

We have been told that Condé has been taken over; we found in this place 1,600 prisoners, 130 guns, muzzle ammunition for six months, 6,000 packets of cartridges, a very large store of gunpowder, 6,000 bombs, 6,000 cannon balls, and this place in good state of defence.

On the same day an English colonel passed in our camp with all his escort and thirty horses, which had been taken in the vicinity of Maestricht by our vanguard. It was in this same camp that we celebrated the surrender of all our towns that the Imperials had delighted us: Quesnoi, Landrecies, Valenciennes, Condé.

Here is the way in which the rejoicing was made in the Army of Sambre and Meuse. The feast was announced at six in the morning by three cannon shots from the positional pieces that were in each division. At half past seven the same pieces repeated the same thing. The music of each demi-brigade was placed on the band's forehead, where they played various patriotic tunes throughout the ceremony. At half past eight a battalion fire was carried out in each division starting to the right of it. This fire finished, the brigadier general passed in front of each battalion, shouting: *Vive la République!* We united with his voice. The distribution of brandy was given to the whole troop. The order has been given that everyone return to their barracks. It was not without needing it, because since midnight we had been under arms.

1st Vendémiaire, Year III.—We left the camp, of which it was the first party *sans culottine*, to approach Maëstricht, and join our vanguard which was under its walls and had fought valiantly.

The city of Maëstricht was blocked off and completely surrounded. We stayed there for a few days, and from there we set off. We crossed the Meuse, above Maëstricht on pontoons to rejoin our vanguard, and go in pursuit of the Austrians. A part of our army remained to contain the garrison of Maëstricht until we had pushed the Austrian Army back across the Rhine. We walked for several days without meeting any vestige of the Austrian Army.

Arrived at a strong river called the Roër, it is there that they hoped to gain the victory and prevent us from passing. They were well entrenched in places where we could have passed. Despite several obstacles that were in front of this river, we did not hesitate a single moment to attack.

The battle was bloody for both parties, and lasted from morning until evening; at night, we made the enemy abandon the river. We have had several hundred wounded men that day. Our position artillery pieces, forty in number, were in the vicinity of the river and never stopped playing; those shooting muskets did the same. The enemy responded to the hell-fire that the Republicans were making. In the evening, when the fire had ceased, we retired back a little into the plain which touches the river, to spend the night. We saw the enemy making great fires, for they were burning their barracks; we judged by that that they were going to flee. It was so: around midnight, they set off.

We worked all night to make bridges with carts, wagons tied with big trees, which were on the edge of the river; we put planks on these constructions and in the morning, at daybreak, we passed in the middle of their entrenchments, which were filled with thighs, arms and

THE TAKING OF MAESTRICHT: 14TH NOVEMBER 1794—14TH BRUMAIRE AN III

whole bodies which they had left without burying them. Several of their poor wounded men cried out for mercy; we took them immediately to the ambulance with our own soldiers.

Our right column had crossed the river before us. We had several days march ahead to reach the Rhine, but no Austrians were in front of us. On the evening of crossing the river, Brigadier General Richard announced the capture of Juliers with twenty-four bronze 27 pieces. Since that time, we have only seen Austrians on the other side of the Rhine, near Düsseldorf.

★★★★★★

Moved by the audacity with which our infantrymen had thrown themselves into the water to force the passage of the Roër, despite the current of the water, the embankment of the river and the entrenchments of the opposite bank, the enemy retreated to Cologne.

★★★★★★

Our last camp was on the plain near the town of Neus. This is the manner in which we conducted the Austrian Army with the honours of war, with great cannon fire. Our passage was not very favourable to us: a continual cold rain, a wind which froze our senses, and no other blanket to cover our bodies than the sky. Our enemy was on the other side of the Rhine, quiet, and we were going to retrace our steps to go and lay siege to Maëstricht.

(*This victory of La Roër, which did honour to General Jourdan and his troops, indeed ensured the complete evacuation of Belgium*).

When we got to this town, we immediately got busy doing the necessary work; we made redoubts to support and respond to any outings they might make. We worked on these works night and day.

Despite their grapeshot, we opened guts within pistol range of their stronghold. We attacked them five times whilst there. We did not lose as many people as we thought to lay siege to such a strong town. Our battalion commander was wounded with shrapnel from a grenade, and also several other officers and soldiers.

Every day, the works continued, and by this means we made the security of the besieged more narrow. The city gardeners had planted a lot of winter vegetables in their gardens; but we were the ones who harvested them. Every morning the enemy found themselves locked up more tightly; if there had not been ditches to impede us, we would have taken them at their palisades.

The works were about to be completed; the town began to be bombed on 12 *Brumaire*; it lasted three days. On the 14th, the city of Maëstricht surrendered at two in the morning. One of the city's senior officers came to the bastions and asked the general who was in command of the siege, so they could surrender. (But there were only thirty days of open trenches. The garrison behaved valiantly. 350 guns and considerable equipment were found in the square.) While they were going to look for him, the gunboats and bombardiers redoubled their fire until they received the general's order to cease it. By the time he asked to surrender, the fire was in a store of oil, bacon, flour, etc. At daybreak, we saw all the *bourgeois* on the ramparts and several brought us bottles of brandy.

We held Maëstricht blockaded for forty-four days. During this blockade, the besieged sent us forty-five thousand balls, thirty-four thousand both bombs and busses, fourteen thousand grenades. They sent all these apples to us in our work, but without it having much effect.

The fire ceased, it took three days to arrange the capitulation. The garrison left the city on 17th *Brumaire*; between ten and eleven o'clock in the morning, the imperial troops left by the gate of Germany, and crossed the Meuse in the midst of the besiegers, who formed the hedge on each side of the road where they were to pass. They came out with the honours of war: drums beating, fuses lit and ensign unfurled. When they were almost at the end of the column, they laid down their weapons in front of us; the cavalry and the infantry carried their sabres. There were troops ready to lead them beyond the camp.

The Dutch troop left the same day, but a little later, because it took time for the French column to come and stand in a hedge on the road by which they were to pass, which was from one end of the town to the other. They also came out with the honours of the war like the Austrian troops. They were taken back to their country by our *chasseurs à cheval,* they kept their sabres like the imperial troops. The officers making up the Maëstricht garrison took their horses and all their luggage.

The City of Maëstricht is very strong; it has a fort which commands it and which defends it. The Meuse floats against its walls, and gives water to its pits; it also has forts which are built in the middle of the Meuse, which defends its approach from the side of Germany. There are in the vicinity large plains very fertile in wheat, barley, oats, potatoes, etc.; it is the frontier of Holland.

It was General Kléber who commanded the headquarters; we were on the left side of the town, under the orders of General Duhesme.

18th Brumaire—We left from around Maëstricht to go to the banks of the Rhine.

20th—We spent in the city of Juliers, a pretty little town with lots of walls; the houses of a rather beautiful construction, the very wide streets. There are also very beautiful plains very fertile in wheat and all kinds of grains; we also drank good beer and harvested very good fruit. This city is the capital of the duchy that bears its name.

22nd—We arrived in Cologne; we camped there when we arrived.

29th—We left this camp to go and stay on the banks of the Rhine in the village called Langel. Our posts were placed on the banks of the Rhine; we were one company per farm, very tight because of the large number of troops that were around. I went to see the city of Cologne; it is very large, well populated, the streets wide; there are a number of bell towers. I noticed that on a very high tower there was a crane painted green. The Rhine floats against the walls, and is part of their trade. The city is not fortified, it is surrounded by a simple very high wall. It was there that the elector made his residence.

12th Frimaire—Leave Hangel to pass to the right of the Logne. Following the banks of the Rhine half a league from the Logne, we are confined to the village called Nille?

We received orders to go to Bonn, supposedly to spend the rest of the winter; we left on the 13th; when we were near the walls of the said town, we received orders to go and camp in the villages a league and a half to the right of Bonn. We arrived in these cantonments on the 17th, in a village called Melheim, located on the Rhine. Our staff remained in this village; our company was detached half a league back to a village called Lanesdorf, situated near large mountains; all the same we were on guard on the Rhine.

What cold we endured being on call in these places! Sentries have died on duty; though they were relieved every half hour. The Rhine was all in ice; for twenty-four hours, we had to fast, because our food was frozen, hard as a rock. I do not want to paint the evils that we have suffered on these different occasions; they would be made to soften a heart of rock. Remember the harshness of the cold of the different winters, the scarcity of food and clothing; that will suffice to say that we have been unhappy.

17th Nivôse—Left this cantonment to go to the village called Keising, half a league from Bonn. Being in this village, I went to see the

Line Infantry 1794

Line Infantry 1795

city of Bonn; I will say that it is very beautiful: wide and very clean streets, houses of a beautiful construction, very bright, beautiful very large squares, a superb castle at the entrance of the city, located in the south and belonging to the elector. The Rhine floats against its walls: it is closed only by small ramparts, very well built. In the vicinity of the city, there are beautiful avenues of chestnut and lime trees, surrounded by beautiful plains.

Being in the village of Keising, we celebrated the anniversary of Capet's death. This took place on 2nd *Pluviose*, at ten o'clock in the morning. The battalion being assembled, we made three discharges and the artillery pieces did the same. This was done in the Army of Sambre-et-Meuse, in our cantonments on the banks of the Rhine.

Recollections of the Year, 1795

We left Keising on 5th *Pluviôse* 1795 (old style). Hateful and tiring day to go to Aix-la-Chapelle (Aachen). As we set out, it was raining; it had been freezing for a long time; that day there seemed to be a universal thaw. Never have French people and others seen such a day, the bad weather lasted the full twenty-four hours. The whole troop was tired. You sank into the ground up to your knees, took three or four steps, and you had to stop to catch your breath; so, several soldiers lost their lives there, and even the horses, with nothing on their backs, had a hard time getting away. We were not in swamps, however, but in gravel fields; we would have preferred to walk in water up to the kidneys, rather than in such a way; but there was no choice; the road had to be used.

We have been in this sad situation from morning until evening at night. Having arrived at a small town called Bruhl, the whole demi-brigade could not stay there. It was night: we had to go and stay half a league from Bruhl, in a village. We took two hours to cover this half-mile; when we arrived, the accommodation tickets were distributed to us, but we had great difficulty in finding them, compared to the night.

The next day the road was more favourable, the frost had replaced the thaw, the night had hardened the road, and in the morning, snow was falling which lasted until noon. We left our accommodations at seven in the morning for Aachen. We stayed on our way to Norwenig, Duren, and Eschviller. In Aix-la-Chapelle, we stayed with the *bourgeois*. We stayed there for a month during which the officers and non-commissioned officers went several times to Général de Division Poucet to learn the theory of warfare

The Army of Sambre and Meuse was then considered to be so little disciplined, among the French, that it was believed that the generals dared not fight any battle for lack of discipline and subordination among the ranks. These slurs all came from the enemies of freedom, who sought to create disorder among our troops, giving birth to the idea that the right of warriors was to plunder any conquered country.

But the Frenchman knew how to behave more valiantly, because it is the discipline which made all our successes, and which excited the admiration of all Europe. This is why the enemies of the Republic wanted to lead us to pillage; the perfidious knew well that an army without discipline is a defeated army; they knew for themselves that brigands are never more than a troop of cowards. We have denied this calumny by our conduct; the love of order and discipline, respect for people and property, will always distinguish the Army of Sambre and Meuse.

Here is a speech by the representative of the people Gillet to the inhabitants of Aix-la-Chapelle, which proves the generosity of the French:

Inhabitants of Aix-la-Chapelle,

Acts of cruelty were committed in your town against French soldiers when the army retired in March 1793: sick and wounded soldiers were thrown out of the windows into the street; others were shot by *bourgeois* who were hiding in their houses. We will not use any rights that just reprisals might give us. If the enemies of France have covered themselves with all crimes, the French will always be honoured to be generous. But the blood of our cruelly slaughtered brothers demands revenge.

Doubtless these acts of barbarism have been disowned by the majority of citizens, and can only be the work of a small number. We ask that the culprits be delivered to us within twenty-four hours; you owe us this justice, you owe it to yourselves on pain of being deemed accomplices in the most atrocious crimes.

Signed: Gillet.

On 10th *Ventôse*, we celebrated the feast of the capture of Holland, and, that same day, the nobles and those who had titles of nobility burned them in our presence, under arms.

★★★★★★

On February 29th, 1795, Holland was indeed conquered and on the

48

following May 16, it signed a treaty of alliance with France which it faithfully observed until the day when Napoleon wanted to impose a king on the nation that the Republic had respected.

★★★★★★

I would say that Aix-la-Chapelle is very large and well populated: there are many manufactures of all kinds; there is good vulnerable water for drinking and bathing; there are beautiful tall houses, beautiful wide streets and beautiful large squares. It is only enclosed by several simple walls; it is a very old city.

We left Aix-la-Chapelle on 11th *Ventôse* to go and settle around Aix-la-Chapelle, in the town called Eschviller; our company was posted to a village called Nolberg.

I will say that in the countryside of these countries, they are quite at ease. They live well with *sauerkraut*, good bacon; their soup is made with hulled barley and salted beef; they eat a lot of carrots, turnips; take a lot of coffee in the morning with fresh butter and jams; their drink is good beer and *chenik*. Their houses are very clean, washed every Saturday; their cookware is in black and yellow iron, very well lightened, and even their rack; tweezers and fire shovel, everything is in the greatest cleanliness. The sex of both kinds is very affable there; men, their costume is no different from ours; but the women have a rather long negligee; for hairstyle, small bonnets of velvet or other colour, edged on the front with gold lace; their hair in several plaits which they roll behind their bonnet like a snail, and held with a large silver pin, as wide as two fingers. In speaking with them German is required. This whole land is very fertile for all things.

We left Nolberg on 25th *Ventôse* to return to the banks of the Rhine; we stayed on our way to Duren, Norwenigbourg, and Bruhl-ville. From there, we went to take our cantonments on the banks of the Rhine, in the village called Nieder-Weslingen. It was the 27th; in this place they reduced our food; we had a pound of bread and an ounce of rice per day; with these provisions we were on foot for part of the night and kept watch from one day to the next. Here is how the supporters of the fatherland had all their comforts.

7th Germinal.—Leaving Nieder-Weslingen. That day we learned about the treaty with the King of Prussia. (*This treaty was not signed until April 5th, 1795 in Basel. Prussia then abandoned all her possessions on the left bank of the Rhine to us.*) Our march was directed towards Coblentz. We stayed, on our way, in Bonn, Breisig, and Kretz. There we stayed for eight days.

49

16th—Arrived in Coblentz where we did not stay; our accommodation was on the left of the city, in the village called Kesselheim, located on the banks of the Rhine.

17th—Entered the city of Coblentz at eight in the morning. We were lodged in *émigré* houses that were all devastated, and we hardly had straw to rest our poor limbs, all heartbroken with fatigue, with our pound of bread and our ounce of rice.

★★★★★★

Marshal Soult was then serving as colonel in our sergeant's division. He also said: "We suffered a lot from the lack of food, to the point that we were forced to reduce the ration by a third". (*Memoirs* , t. I.)

★★★★★★

Many times, you couldn't have bread and very little lean meat; we couldn't find anything for our paper, because nobody cared, and for a three-pound loaf, we had to give twenty-five *francs* in paper.

★★★★★★

Depreciation inevitable as a result of the forced price which caused the fire from 1790 to 1796, for *forty-five billion assignats*. We know that the twenty-four billion still in circulation at the time of the final liquidation were exchanged for *eight hundred million* national goods.

★★★★★★

The city of Coblentz is large and very populated; there are many very wide streets, but also there are some where cars cannot pass; there are beautiful squares and mainly the Place d'Armes, surrounded by stone markers with large iron chains.

Two rows of lime trees form a covered cradle all around the square; it is surrounded by beautiful big houses very tall and of a beautiful construction. And even in a part of the city, when leaving the Place d'Armes, one sees a lawn bowling green and a superb brand new house, which the elector of that city had built; it served us as a hospital while we were in these regions. This house is on the edge of the Rhine, surrounded by large newly planted gardens. There are also wonderful walks. This city is on the north side, bounded by the Moselle which falls thence into the Rhine, opposite the fort, and, on the east, the Rhine floats against its walls. This town had strong bastions and large horsemen who defended its approach, between the Rhine and the Moselle; these fortifications were demolished while we were there, so that it is now only closed with a single wall, on the Rhine side. There is a very tall fort that can burn the city; it is a piece that can only be taken by starvation. The French entered it when they pushed the Austrian Army across the Rhine.

We have built forts and well-palisaded entrenchments half a league from the city between the Moselle and the Rhine, in the plain. The costume of both sexes is the same as that of Aix-la-Chapelle.

5th Floréal—Leaving Coblentz at two in the morning to go to Rhense, a town situated on the Rhine, on the slope of a small hill.— A few days before leaving Coblentz, we were told of peace with the King of Prussia, which gave the whole troop great satisfaction to see that their work was beginning to produce. (See the note of 7 *Germinal*.)

10th—Left Rhense to return to Capellen, on the banks of the Rhine, at the foot of large mountains.

18th—Left Capellen to return to camp on a hill near the town of Coblentz, to the right of the camp called the Chartreuse camp; it bore the name of the convent which was on the end of the mountain, near the city. This convent was completely devastated and was used to stable the horses of the artillery. It is in this camp that we have again done penance. Misery increased every day for the defenders of the country; we were reduced to twelve ounces of bread a day, and many times we couldn't have even that. However, one had to do one's duty, bivouac and stand guard very often. But the spring produced plants to support us a little, which were pea leaves barely emerging from the ground, poppies or *hellfire*, buckwheat, dandelions. With all these pastures, we made a stuffing out of it, which we ate as bread; and when the rye came in kernels, they would cut off its head and roast it on the fire. The barely deflowered apples also served us as food.

It was really a great misery, we saw several soldiers hidden behind hedges, waiting for the ploughman who was planting potatoes split into four to harvest for the next winter, had left his field. Immediately the starving soldiers roamed the field, looking in the ground for small pieces of potatoes, and returned to the camp with their small prey, and cooked them.

★★★★★★

In his *Memoirs* (volume I), Marshal Soult accuses Pichegru "of having left his troops abandoned, neglected and prey to all kinds of deprivation to better promote the execution of the most heinous plan of betrayal." He hoped in this way to disorganise the army. On another occasion, Soult also speaks of potatoes and in very curious terms:

"The army had no other resource to live on than the potatoes that

GENERAL JEAN–BAPTISTE KLÉBER

MARSHAL JEAN–BAPTISTE JOURDAN

were found in the fields. At each stop, the bundles were hardly formed, when the soldiers dispersed around the area to dig up the potatoes. A field was soon harvested, and the meal was soon prepared on the fire in the bivouac. The silence lasted as long as this important occupation lasted: but it did not last long and the provisions were exhausted before the hunger was appeased. The inexhaustible gaiety of the French soldier then returned. Doubting nothing, talking about everything, throwing out original and often even instructive projections, such is the French soldier.

"One evening, while talking about politics and news from Paris, the subject had fallen on the great men who had been brought into the Pantheon or who they had successively been brought out, according to the spirit of the day and the influence of the reigning party. 'Who are we going to put there today?' someone asked. '*Parbleu*', replied his neighbour, 'a potato.' And everyone applauded this projection, which had more scope than the intention of its author had probably wanted to give it." (Soult.)

★★★★★★

Eight or ten days later, we returned to the fields, the pieces of potatoes which had escaped the first search began to come out of the ground; we took them away with great satisfaction at seeing a few small pieces of potatoes to save their lives.

In the morning we beat the drum for the bread, the meat, but we often came back without meat. (The drum was beating as usual the distribution at the appointed time, but this distribution often reduced to nothing or little.)

In the evening, at the start of the night, not every day, we would come back with bread for four men. Everyone left their barracks and gaiety was reborn for a moment in the camp; during the day everyone was as if dead, on his poor straw, patiently taking misery and having fun destroying its vermin.

After such misery and such long and painful evils, some will say: "the soldiers are only thieves. See how they were going to devastate the labours of the poor labourers!" We were well aware of the loss we were causing, but which in such a case could we prefer to die? No, but I believe, to live and to be useful!

In the current of *Prairial*, Year III of the French Republic, the officers, non-commissioned officers and soldiers of the 127th demi-brigade of the Army of Sambre-et-Meuse wrote to the National Convention, expressing themselves in these terms:

What have we just learned? What! the factions are still agitated around the National Representation; the impure remnant of the accomplices of the Terror once again dares to provoke looting, assassination, contempt for humanity, and violation of the rights of the people.

What do these reckless men want? and what are their perfidious plans, their cruel greed? They are looking for pretexts. But it's not bread they're asking for, it's blood. They are jealous of the people's peace of mind, they thirst for their happy future; their villainous rage wants to bury public liberty, under the entwined bodies of the victims, and to dominate this debris.

Legislators, keep the imposing attitude you have taken! Always remember what the people are and that the people do not want to be oppressed by a handful of factions; think that the agitators who dare to threaten you are not citizens of Paris, and that the citizens of Paris are themselves only a small fraction of the Republic!

If the audacity of some grew with their criminal hope, and if the courage of others was weakened by fear; if the former forgot their first duty and the latter their former glory; if it was necessary, finally, for columns to shake victorious armies to go and defend the National Convention; speak, legislators! We fly to surround you, the factions will only reach you by stepping on our corpses.

A republic founded on customs and justice is imperishable like nature.

★★★★★★

This vigorous address in its bombastic form, alluded to the *day of the 1st Prairial* (May 20th, 1795) which had seen the populace of the suburbs of Paris invade the National Convention by killing the deputy Feraud, to the cries of *bread! the freedom of the patriots! the Constitution of 1793!* Fourteen Jacobin deputies paid for this insurrection with their heads, and three months later the popular clubs and societies were dissolved. Each Parisian insurrection placed our generals in a difficult situation, as this letter from the chief who then commanded the Army of the Rhine and Moselle shows; it is framed in truly patriotic terms:

General Jourdan to General of Division Hatry.

Andernach, 7th *Prairial* year III.

I am informed, my comrade, that there was, the first of this month, an insurrection in Paris, and that the people occupied the hall of the Convention almost at eleven o'clock in the evening. However, it appears that at this time the Convention has resumed its sessions. The army must act in this circumstance as it has acted whenever such events have taken place. That is to say, being placed on the frontier to fight enemies from outside, she does not care about what happens inside and she always has the confidence to believe that the good citizens who are there, will succeed in silencing the royalists and the anarchists.

We have sworn to live free and republicans, and we will keep our oath, or we will die with guns in hand. We have sworn to fight the enemies from outside, until peace is made. We will likewise keep our oath, we will remain in our post, and we will fight with as much value as the last campaign. I am sure that these are your feelings and those of the troops you command. But since it is essential to prevent malicious people from spreading bad news in the army, as it is essential to redouble surveillance, so that the enemy cannot profit from the misfortune of our internal quarrels, we must redouble our efforts. zeal and activity, it is necessary that the soldiers of all ranks are always at their posts, that the service of the outposts is done with more surveillance than ever, and that you make sure that the convoys which will pass in the district that you command, are well escorted.

I hope that the attitude of the army will impose it on all the enemies of the Republic.

I will communicate to you daily the consequences of events, and you will have to inform me exactly of the observations which you will make on what will happen in the troops which you command. *Bonjour* and fraternity.

Jourdan.

★★★★★★

On 22nd *Prairial*, we were informed of the capture of Luxembourg. On the 29th and 30th of *Prairial*, and on the 1st *Messidor*, we saw the garrison of Luxembourg pass, numbering twelve thousand, which crossed the Rhine at Coblentz, after having passed in front of us.

On the 9th of the month of *Thermidor*, we received three tricolours with the number of the demi-brigade. With the republicans who made up this body, we swore at this moment never to abandon these flags until death, as we had done previously.

At the same time, we were set on fire with the pieces of the old

55

ones which had been shattered at the blockade of Maubeuge and at the siege of Maëstricht; they look like old warriors who had become quite obsolete as they gained fame and roamed the fields of Bellona.

10th Thermidor—Left the Chartreuse camp in a heavy rain which lasted two days; the orders were given to get us to Creutznach. On the 14th, we lodged, on our way there, in Ventzenheim where we stayed; on the 15th, in Kircheim-Bolanden. In this city, the Prince of Weilburg has a superb pleasure castle; it is surrounded by gardens where there are trees of all kinds, there is a well distributed park: beautiful cascades of water, very pleasant walks, and very well-furnished patches of grass. Sight cannot just examine all of these beautiful things, which seem to be made by nature.

16th—Housed in Pitzersheim. Before arriving at this village, one sees the towers of Mannheim: it is only three quarters of leagues from Neustadt.

17th—In Neustadt; 18th, in Nuzdorff, the first village in France, coming from Coblentz and the Palatine border. (That is to say from the Palatinate.) This village is very large and situated half a league from Landau.

19th—In Altenstatt, a village a quarter of a league from Wissembourg, where we stayed.

21st—In Beinheim, a village on the road to Lauterbourg in Strasbourg. (*The Poncet division, of which our sergeant was part, was to remain in observation with Marceau's division on the left bank of the Rhine.*)

22nd—Left at seven o'clock in the morning to go to Fort Vauban, only the first battalion, the other two were encamped in the plain of Beinheim. We relieved at the fort a battalion of the 92nd Demi-Brigade, formerly of Artois.

This place was called, before the Revolution, Fort-Louis; it could only be taken by famine, but it was delivered to the Prussians in 1792. The French took over this place the same year after the unblocking of Landau. During the time that the Prussians remained at the said fort, they undermined the district and other fortifications.

★★★★★★

On January 19th, 1793, the Austrians and not the Prussians had indeed evacuated the fort by blowing up the fortifications. It was after the lifting of the blockade that the Duke of Brunswick wrote to the King of Prussia this famous letter in which he asked for his recall, saying:

"When a great nation, such as the French nation, is led to great actions by terror of torture and enthusiasm, the same will should govern the *approach* of the allied powers."

★★★★★★

When they had to be abandoned, they blew up all the mines; there were still a few houses where they set on fire when they left, so now this place is like a desert. We were lodged in old hovels, like the whole battalion, because the Rhine had overflowed, and the barracks were still full of water. The bad air which reigned in this place made that all the battalion, and even the two others, were taken of illness; it was like a plague.

Up to ten men per company were obliged to go to the hospital, because they were attacked with a very violent fever. Of the sixty men that we were in our company, we remained two who were not sick. The fever was bad, as many of them died from it. We made our purgatory in this place; night and day we were tormented, there were little flies that we call *cousins*, who gave us great pain, there were some so thick that they would have been cut with sabres; fleas and lice were not lacking.

Being in this place, we made the celebration of the anniversary of the Federation. The 23rd *Thermidor*, (*23rd Thermidor of the year IV must coincide with August 9th, 1795, and the feast of the Federation was celebrated on July 14th, there appears to be a date error*), each piece of cannon fired three shots, and each soldier the same. The rejoicing took place in this way in the Army of the Rhine and Moselle.

12th Fructidor—Got out of the fort; it is on an island, and the Rhine passes all around it. The Prussians had burned part of the bridge which leads to a small fort which is on the Alsace side; it bears its name: this bridge crosses an arm of the Rhine and leads to the great fort: at that time, to enter it, there was only a flying bridge. Leaving this place, we went to camp at the camp near Beinheim. The guards were not re-lieved when leaving, because of the great illness; we were relieved by one of our battalions.

14th—We left the camp to go to Strasbourg. I met an old *bourgeois* who stopped me and said: "My friend, I can't help laughing, given the costume the Republic gives you, because you look more like a Capuchin than a soldier."

I told him that the habit did not make the monk and that he could continue his walk; that he wouldn't be so surprised any more, because he would see a lot of them of that colour. He was not entirely wrong, because I was wearing a brown *capote* that I had received in front of Cologne.

★★★★★★

Nothing is more capricious than the uniform of the armies of the Republic reduced to improvising everything with the only resources of the countries they crossed. At a very early date, moreover, at the siege of Paris in 1870, we saw a mobilised battalion dressed in brown hoods.

★★★★★★

We went to stay with the *bourgeois* when we arrived. On the 15th, we entered the Finkmatt barracks. Left Strasbourg on the 16th; the guards were not relieved on leaving, for there was no garrison.

16th and 17th—We stayed at Plobsheim and Rhinau, villages located a quarter of a league from the Rhine, but all the same our posts were established there. It was in this place that I began to do sergeant-major service.

19th—We took up arms to receive our new Constitution; it was read to us, and being finished, all those who knew how to sign, signed the minutes, to send to the Convention, to prove to them the satisfaction that we had with the work they had just completed for us. We returned immediately.

4th complementary (we know that the republican year, composed of twelve equal months of thirty days, had five so-called complementary days for ordinary years and six for leap years)—Left Rhinau for La Wantzenau, a large village on the road from Strasbourg to Lauterbourg.

1st vendémiaire year IV. (*September 23, 1796*)—Left from La Wantzenau to go to Offendorf, a quarter of a league from the Rhine, on the left of Strasbourg.

28th—Departed from Offendorf for Berg, a village near Lauterbourg, half a league away.

2nd Brumaire—Left Berg, for Woerth, village on the Rhine. In all these places, from Wantzenau to Mannheim, I recognise that the war has indeed caused misery in all the villages and towns; the Imperial Army and ours have not ceased to fight along these borders. The villages are devastated; part of the inhabitants emigrated when the enemy came to the vicinity of Strasbourg.

58

3rd—Left Woerth for Speyer, a large town on the banks of the Rhine, in the Palatinate. This city is closed only by simple walls, but nevertheless surrounded by ditches filled with water; it is a very commercial city surrounded by large plains. Our lodging in this town was in the houses of emigrants which were all devastated; and, to bed, very short straw. We arrived at ten in the evening.

8th—Left Speyer for Otterstadt, still going down the Rhine.

12th—Departed from Otterstadt for Waldsee, a formerly fortified village; now we can still see the old ditches, part of the wall and the arch of the doors.

13th—Departed from Waldsee for Muhlrhein (?), half a league to the right of Mannheim. I went to see this city; it is populated, but it is not very extensive; there are beautiful, wide and very clean streets, and well aligned; the beautiful houses, tall, but not one more than the other; from each crossing we see the rampart at each end of the streets, there is no crossroads.

The streets and squares are very well illuminated: on each side of the streets, at a distance of thirty paces, there is a lamp-post: the square is large, and the house of the Prince of Mannheim is located on the square.

(*It was before 1777, the elector palatine of the Rhine. It was then the Duke of Bavaria*).

The approaches are well defended by good advances and good bastions furnished with strong cannons. At that time, the Austrian Army laid siege to it; the fortifications on the Rhine side are a single rampart. The bridge that crossed the Rhine was made up of fifty-four large boats; the length of this bridge was eight hundred and forty-four feet: there was a fort which defended the approach of the Rhine on this side. But the French demolished it the first time they took this town; they immediately built batteries in the same place to beat the city.

19th—Left Mannheim to retrace our steps, we came to the village of Waldsee where we were on the 12th.

★★★★★★

An attack by Marshal Clairfayt at this time determined the retreat of the Army of the Rhine-et-Moselle, placed by Pichegru in untenable positions, and the place of Mannheim, abandoned to itself, surrendered a few days later. The lines in front of Mainz were forced.

★★★★★★

Being in this village, the Austrians were bombing the city of Mannheim; the fire was in the prince's castle. Our people had been driven back to Mainz: the whole army was retreating. There was still a strong battle in the vicinity of Frankendal; but as the Austrian Army was three times more numerous than ours, it was necessary to give way to them, and to retreat on the town of Landau, and Mannheim was not long in being blocked. We were forced to withdraw to our borders; the Austrian Army crossed the Rhine on several bridges and attempted heavy blows. (*It was double ours which had seen one of its four divisions crushed. The other three withdrew with difficulty, losing almost all their artillery.*)

24th—Left Waldsee to come to the camp near Speyer.

Left this camp on the 29th. As we were in a circuit of the Rhine, the Austrian Army was advancing with great strides; we would have been stranded. They are not trying to make us abandon the Rhine, and their column slipped along the Vosges mountains.

We therefore left the camp at two o'clock in the morning to go to the Guermersheim lines where we remained camped until 9th Frimaire. In this place we ran out of food for five days in a row because of the large number of troops, and there was still no established food administration. During these five days, we ate potatoes that we went to look for under the snow, in holes, in the middle of the fields of cultivators.

(*An armistice was concluded a few days later very timely for the Army of the Rhine-and-Moselle, very reduced in men and horses.*)

9th Frimaire—Left this camp to enter into cantonment at Belheim, a large village located on the lines of Guermersheim.

16th—Left to go to the village of Hoerdt, but we still bordered the lines which ended at the Rhine.

20th Nivôse—Left this village to make a move towards Strasbourg. The same day we went to stay in Auenheim, a village behind the Rhine. Left Auenheim in a heavy rain, with a thaw which made us a very bad road. The 22nd, at seven in the morning; we stayed in Hagenbach, a town, we stayed there.

24th—Left for Neubourg; large village on the Rhine, surrounded by marshes.

28th—Left for Berg, half a league from Lauterbourg, where we had stayed on our way to Mannheim. Being in this village, there came a decree of the Executive Directory so that all the troops of the Republic take up arms on 2nd *Pluviôse*, and renew the oath to be faithful to the French nation and likewise to celebrate the anniversary of our last king of France. This is what we carried out on 2nd *Pluviôse* 1796. I ceased to serve as sergeant-major.

17th Pluviôse—Left Berg for Niderroedern where we arrived the same day.

20th—Left for Sonffeldheim.

21st—Left for Bischwiller, a town five leagues to the left of Strasbourg.

22nd—Left for Reichstett, village on the road, half a league from Strasbourg.

29th—We set out to go to La Wantzenau, two leagues to the left of Strasbourg.

30th—Left to go to the plain near Kirchheim, behind the Rhine and three leagues from Strasbourg. It was the staging area where the 127th and 91st came together to form a single demi-brigade of the two.

Here is how this enrolment was done. We formed two ranks; the rows were opened in each of them; the general of division reviewed it. The ranks were immediately closed; the quartermaster called all the captains, lieutenants, second lieutenants in the centre of the two demi-brigades to draw among them the oldest ranks and place them in their respective camps. It was the same with non-commissioned officers and corporals; and all those who found themselves supernumerary, an auxiliary company was formed. Then the two demi-brigades were broken up by platoons; the 127th joined with the 91st, starting with the first companies, and imperceptibly following. After this mixture, we formed the square to let us know our chiefs. After the whole ceremony has been done.

On this day, the 127th lost its number and was married to the 91st from which it took the name. I saw that when we made weddings, that nothing was missing to celebrate this happy feast; but among us it was not the same, for that day we had no bread. This did not surprise us, because it was not the first time.

Each has gone back to his cantonments; the 5th, the last company in the 1st battalion, at La Wantzenau; and the 1st in Kilstett. That day,

I changed company; I was in the 5th of the 1st (captain Mondragon).

2nd Ventôse—Leave La Wantzenau to join the head of our battalion in the village of Kilstett on the 3rd, to press to the left while going down the Rhine; our first battalion held from La Wantzenau to the Ill along the Rhine. This extent was six leagues; our company was in the village of Offendorf doing service on the Rhine.

17th—Left Offendorf for Weyersheim, where the whole battalion came to quarter for a month; afterwards, we returned to do a fortnight in these same cantonments on the Rhine, and we returned to do a month in the rear. It was done in battalion turns.

21st Germinal—Left Weyersheim to resume our cantonments on the Rhine; we were the same in Offendorf.

26th—Having left Offendorf to go to the Haut-Rhin Army, we stayed on our way to Hoenheim, a small league to the left of Strasbourg. The next day, the 29th, in the morning, we spent in Strasbourg and we stayed in Erstein, town; on 30th *Germinal*, in Kuenheim; the 1st *Floréal*, in Andolshein, a village two leagues to the left of Brisach and a league from Colmar, to the right; we had stay there.

3rd—In Herrlisheim, located a league and a half from Colmar.

4th—At two o'clock in the morning, left for Ensisheim.

5th—At one o'clock in the morning, left for Huningue. We did not enter the city; we received orders to stay in the surrounding villages. We took the ferry, and we were confined to the village called Attenschwiller on a small hill one league from Basle, on the same side and two leagues from Huningue. Being in this village, we occupied the posts of safeguard of the canton of Basel. No one passed through these posts without being provided with a permission signed by the general-in-chief. If it had not been done in this way, we would have removed part of the food and merchandise from France.

The frontiers of Switzerland were demarcated with large wooden posts at a distance of a third of a quarter of a league; it was inscribed on a tinplate: *Safeguard of Basel.*—This epitaph was inlaid at the top of the gallows.

During the month of *Floréal*, we learned of peace with the King of Sardinia. We also celebrated the feast, on the 10th *Prairial*, of the victories won by all the Armies of the Republic.

★★★★★★

In seven weeks, the Army of Italy had conquered Piedmont, dictated peace to the court of Turin, occupied Verona and Milan, invested Mantua. Disconcerted, Austria took Wurmser and 56,000 men on the Rhine, to oppose them to Bonaparte, and we will see the Army of the Rhine-and-Moselle take advantage of this to resume the offensive.

★★★★★★

This party began at six in the morning. At the same moment, the general assembly was beaten: at eight o'clock we assembled; we were immediately on the ground chosen by the battalion commander for this celebration. We did the exercise for a while; afterwards, we were informed of the victories won by the Army of Italy. It was at this moment that we swore by mutual agreement to support their efforts, and that, following the example of our brothers in arms from Italy, soon the successes of the Army of the Rhine-and-Moselle would equal theirs. We returned to the village with cries of Vive la République! On that day the Republic passed us the bread, the meat, the double brandy. That was the order of the general-in-chief.

13th Prairial—Left Attenschwiller for Hagenheim, in a small hill, and half a league from Attenschwiller and the same distance from Huningue; this village is largely inhabited by Jews.

17th—Left Hagenheim at five in the morning to enter garrison in Huningue. It is not very extensive, but strong by its bastions furnished with large cannons which forbid approaching; the streets are wide and well lit; there are many barracks to house the soldiers; the *bourgeois* houses are not very high, but they do not go beyond each other; the Rhine floats against its bastions and gives water to the ditches. There is a beautiful square which is a good one hundred and seventy square feet, it is surrounded by pavilions which are used to lodge the officers of the garrison. This town is half a league from Basle; at each gate there are three strong drawbridges and good barriers. While we were in the city, we only had straw mattresses and bed wood for any furnishings, but as a reward, there was no shortage of chips.

8th Messidor—Went out at eight o'clock in the evening to go to Ottmarsheim; where we arrived at three in the morning; the village is within gunshot of the Rhine, and on the road from Huningue to Brisach.

9th Messidor—All the cantonments which were to guard the Rhine from Huningue to the lines of Guermersheim, were ordered to take up arms at ten in the evening. It was the night of 5th to 6th *Messidor* that we had chosen to cross the Rhine. Here is the ruse which one employed for this fact: Towards midnight, there were several companies of grenadiers in boats, which crossed the Rhine, where they cut the throats of several enemy posts. The attack was general throughout the whole extent of the line of the Rhine, for the cannonade was heard, as well as the fusillade, from two in the morning until four o'clock. We shouted: Forward such and such a column! let's go! let's get on board! The passage is ours! We made recognisable different regiments of cavalry and artillery to show that we were many people moving. The place intended for the passage was at Fort Kehl, near Strasbourg, where this attack was not taking place, and the enemy did not know where we intended to pass.

★★★★★★

To better surprise still, Moreau had two false attacks executed on Speyer and Mannheim. During this time his right wing, brought quickly to Strasbourg, luckily crossed the Rhine on June 24, 1796, on a bridge of boats prepared in the greatest secrecy.

★★★★★★

It was not where we made the most noise that we wanted to pass.

The passage took place without having suffered the slightest loss; they were so surprised and deceived by our manoeuvres that they took the *commandant* of Fort Kehl with his garrison prisoners of war.

17th Messidor—We left Ottmarsheim at four in the morning to go to Balgau, a village two leagues from Brisach, on the right. On the night of the 18th to the 19th, all the cantonments took up arms to make the same attack as that of the 5th to the 6th.

19th—Leaving Balgau at eight o'clock in the morning to go to Neuf-Brisach, a fortified town where there is a beautiful square surrounded by four entrances, each closed by four drawbridges; the barriers, houses and barracks do not go beyond the first rampart. There is a beautiful square surrounded by four rows of poplars which are cut so that they do not reveal the square outside; at each corner of this square there is a well, and right in the middle of the square one sees the four doors; the streets are well aligned as well as the houses. Under all the ramparts are casemates, and on these casemates is a beautiful promenade that goes around the city. These ramparts are lined with strong cannons; the water comes into the ditches through a channel that comes from the river.

21st—Leave Brisach to go to Marckolsheim, a town four leagues away, on the same road.

25th—Left Marckolsheim at ten o'clock in the morning to go to the vicinity of Neuf-Brisach to make a false attack. It was the night of 25th-26th, near Vieux-Brisach, on an island in the Rhine; a hundred men embarked to cross the Rhine, they put to flight several enemy posts; they surprised one near a battery, they slit his throat. In another, they took a gunner, two carters and three horses. At daybreak, the cannon was heard from right and left on the bank of the Rhine. At around four in the morning, the enemy returned several cannon shots. Around seven o'clock in the morning, the men on board returned and we stopped the attack: it was made to establish a bridge at Rhinau.

28th—We left these cantonments at ten in the evening to go to Brisach, where we arrived at ten in the morning. We moved opposite Vieux-Brisach to cross the Rhine; we passed it on a flying bridge around three in the afternoon of 29th *Messidor*. We stayed in big barracks that the Austrians had built when the French besieged the town of Vieux-Brisach.

These lodgings were covered with earth and behind the Vieux-Brisach, out of gun range.

30th—We crossed the Rhine again at ten o'clock in the morning to go to Huningue; we stayed on our way to Ottmarsheim.

1st Thermidor—Having left at four in the morning, we arrived at Huningue, and we crossed the Rhine around ten in the morning. We went to the first village where wine was distributed to us. From there, we went to stay in Lorrach, a village in the Marquisate. I will say that we crossed the Rhine on a flying bridge, and after that we had to cross an arm of the Rhine with small boats, which took us a long time.

3rd—Left Lorrach at two o'clock in the morning to go to Schopfheim, a small town between two mountains lined with beautiful woods; the hill is lined with beautiful, well-kept meadows and all level where they put the water when they see fit. This place has many factories, both forges, wire factories, paper mills, etc. I will also note that the Austrians had left the banks of the Rhine on 27th *Messidor*, because our column which had passed through Strasbourg was taking them from behind the Brisgau mountains to cut off their retreat.

9th—Left Schopfheim at two in the morning to go to Sackingen.

We crossed the Rhine again at Laufenburg. In this place, the Rhine makes a big jump at the bottom of the bridge; it passes between two rocks, it is extremely fast. The bridges we pass under are all covered and well-constructed. Sackingen and Laufenburg are two small towns near the Swiss borders and located seven leagues from Schopfheim.

10th—Left Sackingen at two in the morning for Eibrechsferengel? We left on the eleventh at two in the morning to go to Fiezen, a village eight leagues away.

12th—Left Fiezen at three in the evening to go to Singen, where we arrived on the thirteenth at four in the evening.

14th—Left Singen at ten in the morning for Esplingen, a village on Lake Constance.

15th—Left on the 15th at four o'clock in the morning to go to the Abbey of Salmonswiler, also located on the lake, in Swabia. This is where we saw the rear guard of an enemy column. Right and left skirmishers were detached to search the surroundings of our route; after firing several rifle shots, they continued their retreat. It was in the abbey, or to put it better in the plain above, that we started to camp. I will say that all the villages which I spoke about above and where we stayed, are located on the borders of Switzerland, coming from Lake Constance. General Férino's column drove the enemies from various places located on Lake Constance, to the right of the Swiss side and seized the town of Brégenz where there were about thirty pieces of cannon of various calibres. (*The artillery indeed numbered thirty-one guns, and the sacks of grain numbered forty thousand.*)

★★★★★★

Milanese of origin and captain in the Austrian service, Férino had come to offer his services to the French Revolution which made him lieutenant-colonel and general in 1792, major general in 1793. The empire made him count and senator; his division consisted at the time of this writing, twenty-three battalions and seventeen squadrons.

★★★★★★

We passed at the foot of Fort Randenburg, situated on a sugar loaf mountain, which is not commanded from either side, which surrendered without resistance; there was found a well-stocked arsenal, forty-three bronze guns, and a quantity of ammunition.

We were under the command of General Palliard. Our column took to the left of Lake Constance; We left the camp near the Abbey of Salmonsweiler on the 16th, at eight o'clock in the morning, in a heavy rain which had started at three o'clock in the morning, to go in pursuit of the enemy. We camped near the village called Eriskirch, at the end of the lake, in a wood where our artillery was forced to fire a few cannon shots. In its surroundings there were several obstacles: ditches, small marshes and woods; but the enemy was forced to retire.

We left the camp on the 19th at four o'clock in the morning to pursue the enemy towards the town of Lindau, part of the region of Swabia. Arrived in this position, as we had followed the borders of Switzerland with a battalion of the 38th Demi-Brigade and a detachment of the 8th Hussars, we left this column on 20th *Thermidor* to join our two other battalions of the 3rd Line Demi-Brigade. We stayed on our way to Waldsee, the city where we arrived at night; we were lodged in a convent where our prisoners of war were held before we crossed the Rhine; but they had been evacuated when we approached. we were lodged in a convent where our prisoners of war were held before we crossed the Rhine; but they had been evacuated when we approached.

21st—Leaving the Waldsee at four o'clock in the morning, we were bivouacked a league in front of the town, and a league from Wurtzack, where we found the two battalions which had crossed the Rhine at Rhinau.

22nd—Left this bivouac at four in the morning to go in pursuit of the enemy which was the Legion of Condé, we camped that same day in a wood part of the Black Forest, near a village named Itett (?) which is part of the circle of Swabia.

23rd—Left the camp at three in the morning to go and camp a league ahead. As we approached, the enemy retired.

25th—Leaving the camp at four o'clock in the morning, we passed through Memmingen, a large and beautiful town, surrounded by small bastions and large gardens all filled with hops; it is with the Duke of Wurtemberg. That same day, we went to camp in front of a village where the *émigrés* came to attack us at five in the morning on the 26th, but they were pushed back with vigour and some prisoners were taken. I have noticed in this region the great mortality of horned animals; it was the plague that was in this country, for none could be saved.

The same day, around six o'clock in the evening, we made a movement to press to the left, to give reinforcement to the third line which had been attacked during the night by the knights of the Legion of

Condé, where they lost many people because in the movement that we made, we saw in places more than a hundred, and many which were spread in the woods, and many were buried which we did not see. Those who were above the ground were men who had partly grey hair.

Their attack was singularly combined, they came believing to surprise our people; when they were within gun range of them, they turned around, and fired the retreating platoon, and their guns were sending shells into the air. Being close enough to our troops to be recognised, our troops immediately fired on these gentlemen. As this little vanguard did not see itself strong enough, it retreated for a while; but immediately they had reinforcements from the 74th which was encamped behind them, and they pushed them back with all the Republican heat. As I said, several hundred bit the dirt. This battle took place on the night of the 25th, in the woods near the village of Obergein. We camped there on the evening of the 26th, we had rain for two days.

29th—Leaving this camp at four in the morning to go forward, we camped on the height, near the village of Meltheim, near a small river and behind a large farm where the general was staying.

2nd Fructidor—Leaving this camp at eight o'clock in the evening to go in pursuit of the *émigrés*, we took the road to the left of Meltheim and we camped in the plain.

4th—Left at eleven o'clock in the morning, we went to camp near an abbey, in Bavaria.

Left on the 5th, at two in the afternoon to go to the camp three leagues from the city of Augsburg, the capital city of Swabia. We were not following a direct route, it was partly side roads; it is a little while since we saw our enemy. We are obliged to walk in long days, yet we could not catch up with him. We were encamped on the edge of a river and in a wood of which I do not know the names, but I will put a name to this camp, and the troops which have camped in this camp will not be able to deny me; I call it the *camp of the anthill*, for there was really not a place where the ground was not covered with them, and all the trees were furnished with them; one could still call it *the camp of penitence* .

7th—Left this camp at six o'clock in the morning, without regret, to cross the river where we found the Austrian Army; on the other side, they had cut all the bridges and were waiting for us on the height.

Although the bridges were cut, that did not stop our march; we crossed it with all the courage possible. As the river was running fast and some Republicans wanted to cross it, there were a few drowned. The depth where we passed was three feet a few inches; we took a quarter of an hour to pass these obstacles. It was on the right of Augsburg, between ten and eleven in the morning..

After this advance, and being on the other side, we formed a column and we marched on the enemy who was forced to abandon his strong positions. Our division took eight hundred prisoners that day and took sixteen pieces of cannon. When they fled, they were pursued four leagues from the city of Augsburg. Our vanguard kept its position, and the army returned to encamp two leagues in front of Augsburg, and a league from Fridberg.

Left this camp at nine in the morning to press to the right and follow the enemy's march, that day we encamped near a village, in the vicinity of a superb castle belonging to an Austrian cavalry colonel. This castle is remarkable for the troops which were encamped in the surroundings; a quantity of beer, brandy and all kinds of effects were found there; the whole house had left when the French Army approached, and everything that was in this house was seized.

10th—Left this camp at ten o'clock in the morning to go and camp half a league away. It was in this camp that we were told of the truce with the Duke of Bavaria.

13th—Left at five in the morning to go to the camp, near Dachau.

17th—Left at six in the morning to go camping in the Munich plain. We had left a certain number of soldiers with an officer in our camp at Dachau, to light fires as if there had been troops. This camp was seen from the heights in front of Munich, it was to show the enemy that we were in force.

We were encamped in the Munich plain near the parks of the Duke of Bavaria. these parks were beautiful and large, surrounded by very high fences and containing all kinds of wild beasts and birds. It was so well built that it was really fun; but war destroys everything; we removed the planks to build shelters in the camp: immediately we began to hunt animals, such as rabbits, hares, roe deer, hinds, stags; the birds did not escape; it was all taken by hand, with sticks.

In the vicinity, to the right and to the left of the city of Munich, the Duke of Bavaria has superb castles, very large and well built; it also has superb parks enclosed by walls, where it has all kinds of animals that one can imagine; there are also beautiful water jets and great avenues, walks etc. Many who have seen them like me have said that it was only the Palace of Versailles that could surpass it; it was all made to enchant.

19th—Leaving the camp at eight in the morning to press to the left of Munich, we camped three leagues away. It was while we were in this camp that the *émigrés* crossed the Isar and came to take an ammunition park which was behind Dachau. We had an ambulance there where our wounded were; they took part of it, our surgeons, our butchers and a company of our demi-brigade which was to guard the park. Those who did not want to surrender, they chopped them; after they had made this capture, they returned to their positions which were on the Ridau, in front of Munich, along the Isar.

(*It was not a corps of emigrants, but six Austrian squadrons detached by General Froelich.*)

21st—Left this camp at eleven o'clock in the morning to go under the walls of Munich, where our vanguard had fought at night on the Isar. So, the *émigrés* wanted to go past Munich; but they haven't won anything. That same day, we camped near the outskirts of this city. The suburbs are large there and there are beautiful houses; the wide streets. The city of Munich is not extremely large, but well populated, the houses very tall, the streets wide and well lighted; in the middle of the square there is a beautiful fountain. It is closed by bastions surrounded by ditches, but it is not in the case of supporting a siege; it is the capital of Bavaria.

In the night battle of the 20th to the 21st that our troops had with the emigrants, we burned tanneries, which were on the edge of the river, and several large timber stores. When the *émigrés* saw that it could not help, they stopped firing. They held a house on the bridge road, which was also burnt down.

The Duke of Bavaria had in the city, for his garrison, at that time, twelve thousand men, both cavalry and infantry.

French soldiers could enter the city with written permission from the colonel. The river that passes near the city of Munich bears the name of the Isar.

The left of our division had already passed the Isar, five or six leagues from Munich, on the right; when we learned of the retreat of General Jourdan who commanded the Army of Sambre-et-Meuse. Our troops were forced to cross the river again and to retire.

26th Fructidor—At one o'clock in the morning we began our retreat, though not being forced by the enemy on our side. We took the road from Munich to Dachau, a town six leagues away; we stayed about four hours under its walls to rest and wait for the left of our division which arrived an hour later. Our retreat started with rainy weather. So, we set off, the whole division, and we came to camp nine leagues from Munich, in the position of 7th *Fructidor.*

28th—Left this position at seven in the morning to perform several movements, on the right of Augsburg and the river. At eight o'clock in the evening of the same day, we returned to take up a position a league from Fridberg, ahead. We were at that moment in the rear, and we even saw ourselves blocked on all sides; we had to fight on all sides and more particularly behind us than in front; it would have been easier to return to Munich than to France.

And who were those who were blocking us? It was a part of the peasants who were used to take our parks, the convoys of sick and poor wounded; they took what they could have and immediately put them to death. They cut us off the roads we had to pass, by large ditches and tree cuttings which they crossed in the road, while the Austrians and the Legion of Condé made us use the rest of our ammunition in order to have more facility to take us.

They believed themselves to be the strongest, but they were quite mistaken, because except that we wanted to get out with all the provisions and convoys, made up of quantities of loaded cars of all kinds, the Imperial Army would not have stopped us for a single day. They had also sent proclamations to all the countries we had conquered, where they told the peasants that the French Army was almost entirely in their power; that they had taken a large part of it between Augsburg and Munich; that there were only three thousand men who had escaped, and that they did not know where to retreat; that is why the peasants hastened to arm themselves against us.

Being in this position, we made several more movements, going towards Munich, but we did not meet any troops.

2nd complementary—We were four leagues away, following the Munich road, and camped near the village of Audelheim.

3rd—Retreated to Fridberg; where we passed the river called the Negel; the same day the bridges were re-established. We did not pass through the city of Augsbourg, we went around it; it has very high ramparts. The same day, we came to camp two leagues on this side, on the road to Gunzbourg.

4th—We left at two in the morning to come to the heights of Gunzbourg where we camped in the ploughed land.

5th—Left at eight o'clock in the morning, we passed in the town of Gunzbourg; we went to take a position three leagues away, bordering the Danube.

1st Vendémiaire, year V.—Left at eight in the evening for the town of Ulm, where we arrived at two in the morning. We crossed the said town at six o'clock to come and take a position nearby. This is where all the parks and convoys have gathered; and the army came to pass so that each division took the march indicated by General Moreau to make an outlet for the passage of convoys, some of the troops were fighting while waiting for the others to join with the parks.

★★★★★★

"This retreat has become famous; however, it must be admitted that it was far from offering the same difficulties as the retreat of the army from Sambre-et-Meuse, with which Moreau had better effected its junction." (Soult.)

★★★★★★

Our position was to the right of the city, which has only small fortifications and is not capable of supporting a siege. We left our position on the 3rd, at half past eleven in the evening, to continue our retreat to Freiburg im Breisgau. We have camped half a league from Ulm; we took the crossing to facilitate the evacuation of our parks.

4th—We arrived near a crossing of the Danube, at eight o'clock in the evening, where the enemy wanted to force our line and cut off our retreat. From morning until nine in the evening, the shooting and the cannon did not stop playing, so that they could not pass. We camped that day in a wood, seven leagues from Ulm. Being in this position, we made several movements both day and night to impose on our enemies.

6th—Leaving this camp at one in the afternoon, we came to camp near a large abbey which is five leagues from Waldsee, ahead.

7th—Left at one in the morning, we went to camp two leagues from Waldsee, on the left.

8th—Left this camp at one in the morning to go to the heights to the left of Ahldorf; this village is located near the large marshes and opposite a park. It was in these surroundings that our column met, so that when the column set out, it was divided at several points, for two or three days; and after there was a rallying point. In this village of Ahldorf a large house burned down overnight.

9th—Left at ten in the morning. The troops, which were marching before us, encountered the enemy, which slowed down our march a little. In the first attack, he made a lot of resistance, but after a few hours of fighting he was forced to withdraw, but without abandoning the road on which our convoys were to pass. Our vanguard advanced and made them abandon their positions. We encamped that day near the village of Berg, quite a considerable height, on the side opposite the enemy, which was on the road immediately near the Abbey of Vincastel, in Swabia.

During the time that we occupied this position near the village of Berg, we made several movements to the right and to the left to enlighten us on the march of our enemies.

★★★★★★

General Moreau, who saw that these movements on the part of the enemy made his retreat dangerous, made them attack on October 1st along the entire line near Biberach, and took away twenty cannons, flags and about five thousand prisoners, among whom sixty-five officers; in this matter, it was General Latour who commanded the Austrians.

★★★★★★

14th—Leaving Berg at eight o'clock in the morning, we came to camp six leagues in front of Stockach.

15th—At four o'clock in the morning, we came to camp on the heights, two leagues from Stockach. It should be noted that we could not go very far because our vanguard had to make an opening among the enemy, and clear the roads to allow our convoys to pass.

16th—Left at five in the morning to camp on the heights, a quarter of a league from Stockach, on the side of the road to Fribourg. It is in these surroundings that we had several convoys of sick or wounded slaughtered.

These poor unfortunates were covered with wounds and helpless. The infamous populace took revenge on them for the plagues of the war which had devastated their country. But what did they gain, these weak spirits who let themselves be seduced by the writings that their lords and their emigrants had sent them, telling them that if they could stop us, the war would soon be over and that they would be freed for two years of any tax?

They were so close that it was only necessary to shake hands to take us, that they all left their cottages and stood on all sides on the road, the paths. Everything was well guarded. The women, the girls, the children, finally all got down to it, and the Austrian Army seconded them in their evil designs.

They came one day to take our powder store which was near this town with several reserve artillery pieces, and also those that we had taken from the enemy and that we had not had the time to evacuate; but they were well received. There were a few of our troops around, they were pushed back and retreated into the surrounding woods. In the villages from which these wretches had left to cut us off, some of their houses were burnt down and others were looted.

We left the Stockach camp after everything was on waggons, and there was nothing left in the store. It was on the 17th, at eleven o'clock in the morning, that we followed the road to Fribourg, and that we came to camp two and a half leagues on this side of Stockach, near a village where all the inhabitants were. gone into the woods to cut our retreat. In this place, we had wounded with their throats cut; during the night someone set fire to a house. Being in this position, we passed in front of the village and we waited for our rear guard.

18th—At one o'clock in the afternoon, we camped on the heights in front of Lemmingen where we were given hope for food; a single man was found in this city and no provisions. About twenty-four houses were burnt; the rain had taken us near the town of Hoch, and the night that we were camping on the heights of the town of Lemmingen was abominable; the rain carried all the earth from our camp up the hill.

19th—Left at one in the morning, we marched through the houses all on fire, and we came to camp on a very high mountain.

20th—Descended from this mountain, to go and camp in the plain near the Danube where the enemy came to attack us around eight in the morning. On the 21st, after several hours of fighting, we pushed them back; afterwards, we continued our retreat. The fight to our right was more engaged than ours, but they could not break through our line which was near the road where our parks and convoys were marching. We continued our retreat, the enemy following us closely, we were obliged, on several occasions, to march in column and to put

74

ourselves in line when there were obstacles where we could not all walk together; some were retreating and others watching.

That day we came to camp near a small town, three leagues from Neustadt; there we arrived at night with continual rain and almost impassable paths.

22nd—Left this position at three in the morning, to come and camp near Neustadt, along the back of the mountain, in a gorge of the Black Forest, on the road to Fribourg.

23rd—Left at noon, we came to camp on the back of a hill, to the left of the road to Fribourg.

26th—Left at ten o'clock in the morning to come and camp in the gorge of Fribourg. Half a league down the road there were large hangars which served as stores for the Imperial Army, and since they were empty, we used them for cover. Our rear guard fought well in this gorge, around Neustadt.

28th—Left at noon, we passed near the suburbs of Fribourg; We immediately went to camp in a gorge on the left of the Brisach road. Our position was near a convent of nuns, which was at the bottom of the gorge.

30th—Left on the 30th, at two in the morning, we took the road to Huningue. Around eight o'clock in the morning, our rear guard was attacked by the enemy, near the suburb of Fribourg. At dawn, we were put in battle formation behind a village located near the road to Huningue and at the foot of the mountain of Fribourg. The morning attack lasted all day; on withdrawing, we camped that day in the undergrowth, along the mountain, four leagues from the town of Fribourg, on the left of the road to Brisach.

1st Brumaire—We took the crossing in the mountains of the Marquisate of Brisgau, Baden country, clinging to the Black Forest. We came to camp on the heights of a mountain four leagues from Huningue.

2nd—We made a movement at eight o'clock in the morning. We came to camp in the bottom of the valley, half a league from the village. We were divided on several points to observe the manoeuvres of the enemy (but in the event of an attack, we met on one point).

3rd—At five o'clock in the morning, the enemy came to attack us on different points; in the first place we pushed back the enemy; he pushed us back a moment later to our position where they took some prisoners. We sustained a long time in the same place, but since they had a lot of artillery in a good position on the height, which gave them a lot of advantages over ours, we could hardly find a place to stand. The continual rain made the ground very muddy, and as there were different hills to guard, in woods where we did not see the slightest light, the enemy only seeking to cut us off our retreat on Huningue (because on the road to Brisach, the cannon was heard, as on our hill, and I believe even louder), the fire was very sustained on both sides all day; we lost a few men, but most of them were wounded. We made several steps to the right and to the left of the hill; a large part of the battalions were in skirmishers when evening came.

We ceded the village in front of which we were. I believe, if that day hadn't had a night, the fire wouldn't have ceased. It was the darkness that made the end of our day. The rain started with the attack and lasted twenty-four hours; towards the end, the powder hardly wanted to set. We might think, as we fought all day, that the enemy has pushed us very far; well, throughout the day we have retreated half a league; that is all the progress of the enemy. For the loss of men, I believe it was equal.

At seven in the evening, we retired. The road on which we had to pass crossed the village which the enemy occupied, and to reach it there were several obstacles, but all the same we had to cross them.

3rd Brumaire.—At seven o'clock in the evening, we set out to join the road: we crossed a wood; from there we went down to the bottom of a very deep hill where we found a river which was about fifteen feet wide and three feet deep; this did not delay our march for long (we were already pierced by the rain of the day), we crossed this obstacle. There was still a small stream at the foot of a rather strong eminence which was lined with brambles and thorns; you had to climb on all fours; and many times, being almost at the top, we fell down again.

At the top we found the road, but a patrol of seven enemy horsemen came to meet us. Our adjutant, named Scherer, immediately shouted to the first: '*Who goes!*'—He answered in his own language: '*Verda!*'—Adjutant to him: '*Prisoner!*'—'*Nix prisoner*'—'*Surrender, scoundrel!*'—'*Nix scoundrel!*'

Immediately he put in his spurs and rode to join his comrades who were even further ahead in the road. Immediately, they came back at a full gallop and passed among us, without receiving a shot, for the weapons were so wet all day and the passage of the river, that they could no longer fire, and then we couldn't see clearly. In the mud up to our calves, we continued our retreat, about two leagues from Huningue. Wet as we were and without food, we camped in the fir trees near the road.

4th—From this position, at four in the morning, we came to the heights near Lorrach to camp. The enemy was on our trail and wanted to pass the Rhine before us, but since the bridge belonged to us, we wanted to pass it before them.

5th—Left at midnight to get to the Huningue bridge around half past five in the morning. When our turn came, at eight o'clock in the morning, we passed the bridge which was built of thirty-seven large boats—we were from General Férino's division during the campaign across the Rhine. During our retreat we had twenty days of continuous rains.

When we had crossed the Rhine again, we went to rest near the village of Bourgfeld, on the road to Basle and Huningue, for five hours. In the evening, we went to stay at Village-Neuf, on the Rhine, half a league to the left of Huningue. While we were on the other bank of the Rhine, we had discovered the old foundations of a fort which was on the edge of the Rhine and near the territory of Basel, we had raised the horn-work and the fort where we had put strong pieces to defend the bridgehead. This work was enclosed by a good ditch full of water; a strong redoubt had also been commanded in front of Huningue, to defend the approach of the newly built fort— These works held the Austrian column back throughout the winter. (*See note further on.*)

As we were back in France, and the enemy was no longer pursuing us, I am going to write a little detail on the costume of the two sexes of Brisgau and the Black Forest.

The situation of the inhabitants of the border is very simple, and they live happily in their little cottages; wood is not lacking, but land is not very common there: they have a little on the tops of some high mountains, where they sow rye with a little wheat; in the valley, they plant potatoes. The pasture is quite cool there, so almost all have cows. The houses are not very thick and made of wood; when a father marries off his children, he builds small houses for them around his own; but they do this when the family can no longer fit in the paternal home.

It is a real desert, so the world that inhabits it is as crude as their dwellings are; most have no education; as nature created them, they remain. The men are rudely dressed, they wear a little straw hat on their heads, their hair short and very spiky; their very strong canvas shirts without collars, because you never see anything around their necks. Their breeches, very wide with pleats all around which make their knees as big as their heads, are gathered like a purse. They wear nothing on their legs, and, on their feet, they have shoes as hard as wood; the soles are two fingers thick, and edged with large nails all around. They have vests that fall to the middle of their thighs; shorter clothes that are buttoned all the way; and the pockets flap at the bottom of the belly. This clothing is all in canvas, most of the time all black; also, they look like charcoal burners.

The headdress of women and girls is a little straw hat with four horns, like a kind of *carquelin. (The small cake that actually has this shape.)* They wear their hair in two braids pulled very close to the head, which is as big as that of a two-month-old calf; a neckline of the same; their throats are adorned with a thick shirt, embroidered with thick lace, with a red corset in which are locked up very large charms, which they bundle up like a bundle. The skirts they wear are of different colours: they put on three, the largest does not pass the knees, the second a little higher, the third goes below the navel; they are each embroidered with a wide braid of different colours. Most often they all go barefoot; they have high shoes with strong nails. Their food is milk, bacon and *sauerkraut*. We stayed in their houses on our way to Lake Constance; they always had their eyes on us.

In Brisgau, the people are not so rude, nor the costume either; the land is more fertile there and there is still fine rye, but the fashion for the costume is hardly different

6th Brumaire—Left the Village-Neuf at noon to come and stay at Grand-Kembs, a village half a gunshot from the Rhine, three leagues to the left of Huningue, on the road. During our retreat, we had twenty days of continual rain.

14th—Leaving Grand-Kembs to press on the left at eight o'clock in the morning, we stayed in Sausheim, on the 15th, in Blodelsheim; on the 21st, with four companies, stationed at Fessenheim. These villages are between Huningue and Brisach, on the road following the Rhine.

25th—Left Fessenheim to come and quarter in Biesheim, the

whole battalion. This village is half a league from Brisach, on the left.

7th Frimaire—Left Biesheim at eleven o'clock in the morning for Witternheim, seven leagues from Strasbourg and two leagues from the Rhine.

11th—Leaving Witternheim, we came to stay in Nordhausen, four leagues from Strasbourg.

12th—Went out at two in the evening to go to Fort Kehl. There, we relieved the 31st Demi-Brigade which was encamped to the left of the fort, on an island in the Rhine. The 31st relieved us after three days: so that every three days, we got up to the line, until the time of 30th *Frimaire*, when we started to get up every four days because the cold was no longer so hard. But also, the more often we got up, the more people we lost, for the enemy was firing constantly, night and day; it seemed like a thunderstorm.

When we were relieved, we would spend as many days in the village of Bischheim; there were two leagues of way to cross the bridge and reach our camp, which was two leagues from Strasbourg, on the left.

9th Nivôse—The general assembled the officers of our battalion (which was the first), and led them on the right of Kehl to show them the entrenchment of the enemy which we were to remove during the night. The said officers took the necessary measures to lead their companies on the ground, and to accomplish this task. All obstacles were foreseen; they told their companies what to do during the night. We made the distribution of new cartridges and grenades; and immediately a ration of brandy by each man at midnight. At that moment, the companies were assembled in the utmost silence, and the battalion immediately set out to go to the land which was half a league from our camp, to the right of the fort, where we arrived at two in the morning.

Being opposite the entrenchment that we were to take, we were trained in battle at pistol range, we were made to carry to the right and, at the same time, we stood up and we went on the entrenchment of the enemy by carrying out platoon fire; it was taken from them without much resistance on their part, and some prisoners were taken. As for the number of wounded and dead, it was only known from deserters who reported that in this affair they had about 400 men *hors de combat*.

We withdrew without being forced; we came behind our entrenchments: we left the places as we had found them. Our battalion lost forty-eight men both killed and wounded in this affair. This took place on the 10th at three in the morning and we returned to our camp at half past six in the morning. Our other two battalions did the same over the following days, but with fewer casualties.

We continued to serve in this area until 20th *Nivôse*, when we were relieved at four in the morning. For since the Austrians had taken an entrenched camp from us which was to the right of the fort, their grapeshot was destroying everything they saw on the bridge at daybreak. They made a fire with their cannons so that the earth trembled. Between seven and eight in the morning, there were four broken boats on our deck. At that moment, a parliamentarian came to the general who commanded the fort and summoned him to evacuate. The generals assembled, and seeing themselves unable to keep the said Kehl any longer without losing many people, because of our enemy's guns, agreed that we were going to evacuate the fort. It was done within twenty-four hours, from 20th to 21st *Nivôse*; and the troops of the emperor took possession of it according to the arrangements agreed upon between the two powers. On leaving Kehl, we came to stay in our ordinary camps which were in Bischheim.

I will say that this siege gave us a lot of trouble. The harshness of winter seemed to assist our ills; the snow and the icy rain were heavy on our light clothing, and that was the weather during this siege. We should be well used to the cold; we were camped on the sand and we could not have wood to make our soup; we tore up some small roots from the ground which made us rather smoke than fire; really it was misery and compassion. Our pay was several months in arrears and we were not getting a penny.

★★★★★★

Nothing is exaggerated in this account of the situation. "Wanting to stay within reach of Alsace to take advantage of the intrigues that Pichegru continued to hatch, and for which he had even returned in person to Strasbourg, the Austrians began with the siege of Kehl. Some work had been done there during the campaign, and an entrenched camp had been established ahead, but all these works were simply earth and seemed unlikely to hold up for long against regular attack. Nevertheless, the defence was such that it withstood *forty-seven days* of open trenches, leaving the enemy with only heaps of broken earth. It was the same at the head of the Huningue bridge, the works of which were still smaller, and which, attacked since the first days of November, was not evacuated until the following February 2. These

two memorable defences have been described in special works."—
(Soult.) See no. 3 of our Supplement.

★★★★★★

It was during this quarantine that the true Republican distinguished himself, holding his rank there with bravery, despite the harsh
weather of the winter season and the misery that stabbed us on all
sides. Yes, many citizens will say it like me, without compromising
themselves, that it is in this post of honour that we were able to know
the real soldiers, and the love they had for the maintenance of their
country. The place was perilous. A little frozen bread was all our food
there, this place did not allow us to find wood there to be able to
warm up a little our poor limbs, all heartbroken with the cold at the
bivouac.

For us, poor heroes, clothes and shoes had been lacking for a very
long time, without being able to have any; and most of us having no
money to help ourselves in any way; because it had been three months
since no pay had been received.

After having mentioned our generous warriors, I will speak of
those who had, in this moment, so cowardly abandoned their flags
to return to their homes. They took advantage of the moment when
their homeland most needed their services to carry out their projects.
It was not the most miserable soldiers who did this; it was those who
had led a brigand line across the Rhine, who had pillaged and mur-
dered peaceful men in their homes. They had money in their hands,
which is why they fled from the enemy. But these cowards were little regretted, we looked at it as poison coming out of the body of a
man who was poisoned, and they made themselves unworthy of the
French name, and of the esteem of their comrades. I know that there
are not many citizen soldiers who do not wish to return to the centre
of their families, but finally it will be by leaving lost sheep, that we will
submit to the peace of proud men.

They know very well that this peace would be useful to them, but
will they ask for it when they see the disunity in our troops? No! I
believe that only unity and firmness in our companies will force them
to ask us for peace.

It was during the month of *Frimaire*, Year V of the Republic, that
desertions for the interior of France were frequent in the Army of
Rhine-et-Moselle.

Kehl was a beautiful little town, very commercial; during the siege
it was shaved from top to bottom; the *bourgeois* having come home

81

there, did not recognise the location of their houses.

We maintained the Austrian Army during part of the winter, where it exhausted part of its forces. This siege was supported by our army to assist the capture of Mantua which was blockaded by the Army of Italy, a long time ago, and Prince Charles could not bring it help.

24th Nivôse—We left our cantonments around Strasbourg at seven in the morning; we went to stay in the village of Obenheim, located five leagues from Strasbourg.

25th—Left at four in the morning to stay in the village of Bootzheim, four leagues from Brisach.

29th—Left at eleven o'clock in the morning to take our battle line at Artolsheim, a village four leagues from Brisach, to the left on the road. Being in these cantonments, we bordered the Rhine.

25th Pluviôse—Left to go to Sundhausen, a village one league from the Rhine, without doing any service there.

5th Ventôse—Went out to the village of Westhausen. It was a commissioner of the executive power of the canton who made us go there, supposedly that he did not want to pay his contributions. This village is located half a league from Benfeld, on the left, near the road to Strasbourg.

6th—Left at eight o'clock to return to our cantonment at Sundhausen.

10th—Left at five in the morning to stay in the village of Artzenheim, one league from Markolsheim on the Rhine.

17th—Left, we went to lodge in Biesheim, a village half a league from Brisach, where the whole battalion was assembled. We left on the 19th to go to Wihr, a village located three quarters of a league from Colmar.

22nd—Leaving Wihr to stay in Colmar. During our stay in this town, we reviewed General Schauenbourg, who was for the moment inspector general of all the Rhine-et-Moselle infantry. We were five days to spend it. On the evening of the 23rd, each captain was placed by his seniority in rank in each battalion; so that Mondragon's company, which was the fifth of the 1st Battalion, became the third of the 2nd; the other days were spent doing the big manoeuvres with the 56th Demi-Brigade.

27th—Left to go to Wettolsheim, behind Colmar, at the foot of the mountains. Being in this village, we went twice to carry out large manoeuvres with the 56th Demi-Brigade, in the meadows near Colmar. On 3 *Germinal*, we carried out the fire drill, the two demi-brigades together; each soldier had fifteen shots to fire. After these major manoeuvres we returned to our cantonments.

5th Germinal—Lodged in Reguisheim, a village three quarters of a league from Ensisheim, on the left.

6th—Cantoned at Blodelsheim to do service on the Rhine; this village is three leagues from Brisach.

27th Germinal—Left Blodelsheim on 27th *Germinal* to cross the Rhine. The posts on the banks of the Rhine of all our cantonments were not relieved: we left them as they were, and we took the road behind the Rhine. We went to lodge the same day at Sainte-Croix, five leagues from the Rhine; on the 28th in Merckviller; on the 29th at Châtenois, a village in the mountains, near Schelestadt; the 30 in Nordhausen.

1st Floréal—We arrived at Kilstett: place designated for the assembly of the Army of Rhine-and-Moselle. We camped when we reached an island near the Rhine, on the right of the village. The night of the 1st to the 2nd, at four o'clock in the morning, we received orders to cross the Rhine. From the 1st *Floréal*, we had worried the enemy in different places on the Rhine, so that he would not suspect in which place we had to pass, which made our passage easier to carry out, and with less losses. We therefore, despite the great resistance of an Austrian column, crossed the Rhine at four o'clock in the morning, on 2nd *Floréal*.

Having reached the other bank, and the enemy having withdrawn to several islands in the Rhine, favoured by very thick woods, we disputed for two days with incredible intrepidity. But, after such a long fight, the enemy was forced to abandon their positions, after having suffered considerable losses, both wounded and killed or prisoners; they were completely routed.

We also experienced some losses in this passage; among others two wounded generals.

★★★★★★

The wounded generals were three in number: Desaix, Duhesme and Jordy. All had paid in person to double the momentum of the troops in these two beautiful days. Arrived from Paris the day before, the

GENERAL ANDRÉ PONCET

GENERAL GUILLAUME PHILIBERT DUHESME

general-in-chief had thrown himself into the water up to his waist to help, by pulling on ropes with Desaix and his staff, to free a blocked boat. Duhesme had had his hand pierced by a bullet while beating on a drum with the pommel of his sabre to bring back a battalion to the charge.

★★★★★★

But the republican soldiers, who did not succumb to the blows of the enemy, knew how to take revenge for the misfortune befalling their brothers in arms; we made them see that if we were less in number, we were no less courageous.

3rd Floréal.—They abandoned the Rhine five leagues away, leaving us part of their artillery and baggage; and without the woods which favoured their retreat, the whole column would have fallen into our power.

This passage was carried out in broad daylight and by force, the enemy being ranged in line on the other bank. 20 pieces of cannon, several flags were taken from him and three to four thousand prisoners, including two generals.

(*Only General O'Reilli had been taken prisoner, but General Staray had been killed, which explains the apparent exaggeration of the figure.*)

The fort of Kehl, in front of which Prince Charles had exhausted his forces, was taken over by the French after a resistance of a few hours on the part of the enemy.

(*The fort was taken by some dragoons of the 17th regiment who crossed the Kintzig; we were in the process of rebuilding it on a new route.*)

While the conqueror of Italy was stipulating the preliminary articles of peace, the armies of Generals Hoche and Moreau drove the enemy out wherever he dared to dispute the ground.

4th Floréal.—At four o'clock in the evening, we reached the town of Offenburg, where we arrived at eleven o'clock in the evening.

At eight o'clock in the morning, General Bonenfant received a letter from the major general, which was to announce to his brothers in arms that an armistice was concluded with the Austrian Army, and that from that day hostilities were to cease between the two armies; but that their posts would always be kept as they were established, until peace was made.

That day, we received the order to quarter the troops, and around five in the evening, we left the camp in front of Offenburg, to go and quarter in the surrounding villages, on the right. Our second battalion was in the village of Weier, a league away

6th—Went out at five in the morning to camp in front, in Offenburg.

7th—Left at nine o'clock in the morning to stay in the hamlets of the Black Forest, two leagues to the left of Offenburg.

9th—Left at five in the morning to come to the village of Odelshofend, a league ahead of Kehl. All the time that we were in this village, we were going to demolish the entrenchments that the Austrians had built for the siege of Fort Kehl; these works were immense; added one after the other, it would have been fifteen leagues long. We have given way to another demi-brigade, each taking their turn.

20th—Lodged in Ortenberg, a league in front of Offenburg.

23rd—Cantoned in Ottenheim, a quarter of a league from the Rhine and two leagues from the small town of Lahr belonging to the Margraviat. This principality had been neutral since the year IV or 1796.

1st Prairial—Left at four in the morning to go opposite Rhinau to cross the Rhine on a flying bridge which had been re-established. It is there that the demi-brigade assembled, and at the same time crossed the Rhine; it was lodged in Herbsheim near the village of Benfeld, four hours from Strasbourg.

2nd—Cantoned in the village of Roderen, two leagues from Schlestadt, at the foot of the mountains.

3rd Messidor—Went out to garrison at Neuf-Brisach and stay on the banks of the Rhine; on our way there we stayed in Wihr, a village one league from Colmar.

4th—Left at seven o'clock in the morning, we came to stay in Biesheim, a large village half a league from Brisach. We entered five companies from the second battalion and five from the first garrisoned at Brisach.

On 5th *Messidor*, at ten o'clock in the morning, the supply of our barracks was not very brilliant: it was straw on the pavement and some blankets.

5th Thermidor—Being in this city, we celebrated the feast of the anniversary of the revolution. The party started at six in the morning. We beat the *général* throughout the city; at half past six the *assembly*;

86

then the *reminder of the oath.*

A detachment of gunners was sent to their pieces, near the Strasbourg gate. The whole garrison took up arms, as well as the National Guard, and all went to the square to form in the square, in front of the altar of the fatherland, which had been built the day before on the side of the gate of Basel. The procession arrived in the square at seven o'clock: the march was opened by a squad of cavalry from the National Guard; then the drums and the music. Afterwards, came a company of grenadiers of the National Guard with ours; after, it was our colonel, the commander of the place, the municipality of Brisach and the neighbouring villages, decorated with their scarves. To bring up the rear, it was a platoon of infantry and a cavalry of the National Guard. When they entered the square several siege cannon shots were fired.

A number of our officers, the municipalities and several *bourgeois* of the city ascended on the altar of the fatherland; being assembled there, one of the members made a speech, which fully recalled the manner in which the French Revolution had taken place, and how the priests and the *émigrés* had gone about making a counter-revolution, which we had been able to thwart, but that we had to be always firm in our opinion to support the new constitution.

This was the wish of the garrison: we had not made so many sacrifices to abandon our homeland to vile tyrants. It must be said, however, that the joy was not general, because of the sorrows we suffered. This feast was however glorious for the French, but the support of the country lacked what was strictly necessary; the pay was several months in arrears, no clothes were being delivered, and almost everything was lacking. This could well cause melancholy to reign among the troops; so, the party looked like a funeral. The end of the speech ended with: '*Live Free or Die!*' and '*Long live the Republic!*' These cries were only repeated by those who were on the altar of the fatherland; then we started the hymn of the *Marseillaise* which was repeated by our music, but the voices were not unanimous, and that ended the affair.

The procession was returned in the same manner as it had been brought, and the garrison returned to their quarters. At nine o'clock in the evening the same day, our music went to the square where they played different tunes. At the same time, the artificers started fires in the air and several chestnuts were heard, and several other rockets were sent among the spectators who were in the square. The latter meandered through the world, which provided the most entertainment of the whole party; the women, who are usually so curious, fled at the sight of these rockets, for they feared it would get under their skirts. After that, the officers of the garrison gave a ball to end the party.

11th Thermidor—We left Brisach at eight o'clock in the evening to go to Ammerschwihr, a village three leagues from Colmar, to the left, at the foot of the mountains. We got there at five o'clock in the morning, on the 12th. The whole country was attacked with a great disease on horned beasts, like cows and oxen. Villages were entirely depopulated of these cattle; no cure could be found for this disease, which greatly afflicted the inhabitants and the farmers. All these mountains are only vineyards which are of great value; there are also many fruits of all kinds. At the bottom of these villages, coming to the Rhine, there are beautiful plains, which are quite fertile in all kinds of grains and potatoes.

10th Fructidor—Left at four in the morning to go to the Rhine, to the village of Baltzenheim, two leagues from Brisach. Arrived the same day at ten in the morning. In this village, we learned that the conspirators of public unrest and the betrayal of Pichegru, who had commanded the Army of the North where he had won such brilliant conquests, had been discovered.

★★★★★★

Pichegru's intelligence with the enemy had started in 1795, and his premeditated false manoeuvres then compromised Jourdan's army. Deported in 1797, he escaped to ally himself openly with the enemies of the country, and return to die shamefully in Paris. The price stipulated for his treason included an infinite number of articles: the government of Alsace, the rank of marshal, two large cords, twelve cannons, the castle of Chambord, the land of Arbois, a million silver and two hundred thousand pounds of annuities. While awaiting the fulfilment of these promises, the English minister of Switzerland made him pass subsidies. Moreau, who had been provided with written proof of this pact, was accused of having disclosed it too late.

★★★★★★

He wanted to lose in a moment what was costing us so much trouble; he wanted to deliver our strongholds to the Imperialists and to Condé, who wanted him alone to make the counter-revolution in France. But also, the betrayal of Pichegru was lacking, thanks to all our armies which had petitioned the Executive Directory, which revived the hearts of the good republicans when they saw that the armies were still for the good party.

The 1st Vendémiaire year VI—Day which was no longer to be devoted to the Republic, according to the plot of the conspirators. We celebrated with great pomp the feast of the anniversary of the founding of the Republic. Here is the detail of how we celebrated it.

This feast was announced the day before at sunset by a positional artillery discharge, and the next day such a discharge was made at sunrise. Around ten o'clock, the *général* was beaten in all the places where there were troops; each took up arms and went to Brisach Square. Our grenadiers were with the Brisach National Guard which was made up of two companies and two cavalry platoons. Our music and all the drums were opening the march of the procession which was composed of generals, brigade leaders, officers and civil authorities from Brisach. The march was opened by a platoon of cavalry, and, afterwards, a platoon of grenadiers; then the drums and the music. Then a company of *Chasseurs à Pied* from the National Guard, which was made up of very educated little boys of ten to twelve years old, came next. Then, about sixty young citizens of the same age walked in two rows; they were dressed in white, with a tricolour ribbon as a scarf and held in their hands bread baskets, filled with flowers, oak and olive branches.

Four little boys, also dressed in white, walked in front and wore between them a large wreath of oak, laurel and olive tree surmounted by a cap of liberty. Then came the generals, the municipality, the commanders, the officers, then a platoon of line grenadiers and the national guard; then a fairly large number of men from fifty to sixty, armed with pikes. A platoon of cavalry brought up the rear. All the troop and the procession returned in this order to the square, in front of the altar of the fatherland which had been established in the morning. This altar was built from behind with oak branches; it was twelve feet in diameter; the balustrades were covered with carpets of different colours; on the altar were placed vases filled with incense, with the goddess in the middle.

On the corner in front of the altar were raised marble *pilasters*, after which were attached eight white flags on which was painted an inverted urn with the royal staff; on others was a Capuchin holding a cross in one of his hands, and in the other a fiery torch; on the top of the pilasters was a tricolour and a liberty cap.

The main members of the procession ascended the altar, and one of them gave a speech on the founding of the Republic, after which young citizens who were seated in front of the altar sang a Republican hymn. This done, the troops marched from the square to reach the city's glacis, to the right of the Porte de Strasbourg. When the troops arrived at the designated place, several artillery discharges were made. The troops being ranged in line, the general had them put in divisions, in columns; then he gave us a speech congratulating us on our bravery and fearlessness, urging us to continue. It was at this point that he renewed his oath to be faithful to the new constitution; the whole troop also promised. At that point, he had the column deployed to make battalion and file fires; the cannon did the same; each soldier had twelve shots to fire. After these fires ended, the whole troop returned to their quarters.

At eight o'clock in the evening, three cannon shots were fired. A detachment armed with grenades went to the fireworks which was between Vieux-Brisach and Le Neuf. On the glacis, the whole troop attended unarmed, as well as the entire population of Neuf-Brisach and the surrounding area. This fireworks display lasted an hour and a half. When the fire was over, everyone returned to their homes. To celebrate this feast, there were two battalions of our demi-brigade, a company of light artillery, a company or two of heavy cavalry.

We did the Brisach place service for a while. Those who were in the city came to relieve those who were in the villages on the bank of the Rhine, and those in the villages returned to the city, because the garrison was not good. Straw on the pavement and blankets were used for sleeping; in winter it was cold, and in summer it was full of fleas; but in the villages, although they were poor, people were still better there. We were one company per village depending on the service available on the Rhine.

17th Vendémiaire—Leaving Baltzenheim to garrison at Brisach, we arrived there at seven in the morning. We were told that the Army of Sambre-et-Meuse and that of the Rhine-et-Moselle were no more than one, which was called Army of Germany, commanded in chief by Citizen Augereau.

Details of the feast which took place on 30th *Vendémiaire* Year VI of the French Republic. We celebrated it at Neuf-Brisach, in honour of General Hoche, one of the great men the Republic has lost. He died near Paris.

★★★★★★

Marshal Soult said a lot in a few lines on the possible causes of the too sudden death of Hoche: "However, the republican spirit was still very lively in the ranks of the army; also, when the struggle was engaged between the majority of the councils and that of the Directory, this one called the army to its assistance. The bad example was given of having troop addresses made. General Hoche was in Paris, and two divisions of Sambre-et-Meuse were made to advance in the environs of the capital, under the pretext of sending them to the coasts of the Ocean. This movement took place without the knowledge of Director Carnot and of the Minister of War himself, at least the latter made the declaration. General Bonaparte was more circumspect than General Hoche; he confined himself to sending General Augereau to Paris, who helped out on 18 *Fructidor*.

"As for General Hoche, he probably noticed at the last moment that he would not play in the planned *coup d'état* the role which he believed should belong to him and that he would be associated there with whom it did not suit him to be confused. He therefore hastened to rejoin his army, but hardly had he arrived at his headquarters in Wetzlar, when a short illness, the nature of which seemed rather extraordinary, took hold on September 19 (third additional day).

"Rumours of poisoning first circulated: suspicion was based on the fact that General Hoche was probably the repository of important secrets, and that there must be people interested in his ceasing to offend them by his superiority, and the ascendant which it exerted on its army, neighbour of France. Suspicions of such a serious nature cannot be lightly admitted, and it is more than likely that they had nothing to do with, yet they were never cleared up. Anyway, the most sincere regrets accompanied him to the tomb and, to perpetuate the memory, the army had a monument erected in the plain between Coblentz and Andernach, where his body was deposited.

"General Hoche possessed the qualities which constitute the great captain, and he brought them out with the most attractive exterior gifts. His noble and majestic bearing, his open and considerate physiognomy, attracted confidence at first sight, as on the battlefields, his whole attitude commanded admiration. A quick and sure look, an enterprising character that no difficulty was able to stop, very high feelings, and at the same time, a great kindness, a constant concern for the soldier: it was not necessary, not so much that the army might love in him a leader who had always been happy, and who had the glory of having pacified the Vendée.

"He was criticized for ambition. He was only thirty years old when death took him from France; at this age, at the head of an army, with the reputation it enjoyed and the feeling that it had of its own worth, it was very difficult to protect oneself from ambition, especially when he saw the reputations rising at his side which he believed he was capable of matching. So, I believe that if Hoche had lived, he would

91

have warned the 18th *Brumaire*, or at least that he would have taken on the role of Pompey, when the new Caesar came to seize the supreme power."

★★★★★★

This celebration of recognition was announced the day before by several artillery discharges; the next day, the 30th, at six o'clock in the morning, an artillery discharge took place every quarter of an hour; the city bells were rung for an hour. At ten o'clock, the civil and military authorities assembled and went to the communal house where everyone was to meet. When everything was ready, we set off; the procession was opened by a detachment of cavalry from the National Guard, then came the old men ranged in two rows; the first to walk at his head carried a banner on which was written: *Our children will follow his example.* Walked after them young women dressed in white, a crepe in a scarf; a little boy of seven to eight years old carried a banner, on which was written: *He was a good father and a good husband.*

After them walked a number of young girls of eight to eleven years old, also dressed in white; they carried in their hands, garlands of laurel and oak, and little baskets filled with all kinds of flowers. Afterwards came our music which played funeral airs; next came a triumphal chariot drawn by two mouse-grey horses with mourning harnesses; in the four corners were placed four young citizens aged from eleven to twelve, well dressed, combed in hair, with a garland of roses above; a very wide, tricolour ribbon, placed in a sling.

These four citizens each carried a banner, on which was inscribed:

1st *He was to be the Bonaparte du Rhine*; 2nd *Immortal after his destiny*; 3rd *He inspired terror in kings.—His enemy flees before his valour.*

In the middle of the chariot was placed in effigy the coffin covered with a funeral sheet; in one end was written: *here lies Hoche.* His portrait was at the bottom of this sign; in the middle of the said coffin was placed a hat edged in gold, with the tricolour plume which is the style of our generals. The corners of the funeral sheet were held by the four oldest on duty, taken from the officers and soldiers alike. The cripples who were in the depots which were in Brisach followed the chariot. Then came the black veiled drums, which occasionally played dark rolls. Next came the generals, garrison officers and civil authorities; there was a detachment of a hundred men forming the hedge, and a detachment of grenadiers which followed the procession in two rows;

92

the rest of the troop were unarmed.

After having made the tour of the city within, the whole procession was led to the church; the coffin effigy was placed on a homeland altar that had been prepared, and all around it was decorated with tears. The music played several funeral tunes. Then we were given the details of the funeral in Paris, and how all the communes of the Republic were to celebrate a celebration of gratitude for General Hoche. This speech finished, the young citizens sang several funeral and republican hymns. Then our demi-brigade leader made a speech in which he recalled several features of the bravery of Citizen Hoche; then the music played several times, while all the young citizens carrying garlands, laurel wreaths and oak branches, put them around and over the coffin. This was on display for several days in church, and everyone retired to their lodgings.

At the same time, we learned about peace with the emperor. It was on 5th *Brumaire* (October 27th), by a letter from Vieux-Brisach, which had been sent to the commander of the Austrian troops who were for the moment in the principality of Margraviat. This letter said that peace had been made with the French Republic since October 17th, 1797.

(*It is indeed on this date that the Treaty of Campo-Formio was signed.*)

We learned it again from the gazettes which came from Paris on 12th *Brumaire*.

This peace was published to us on 25th *Brumaire* (15th November), at ten o'clock in the morning, in Neuf-Brisach. There has been no celebration for the moment; the feast was postponed to 30th *Nivôse*, it was celebrated with all the pomp possible, according to the preparations.

1st Frimaire—Left Brisach to go to our cantonments on the Rhine line; our company was still in Baltzenheim.

1st Nivôse —We left our cantonments to go to Neuf-Brisach to relieve our four companies.

25th—Left Brisach, to go to Strasbourg, all the demi-brigade. We stayed on our way there, on the 25th, in Schelestadt; the 26th in Erstein, the 27th in Strasbourg; there we received orders to go and stay in villages three or four leagues from Strasbourg, on the left; on the 28th, we were each in the villages that were assigned to us; our company was at Kirchheim, three leagues from Strasbourg.

6th Pluviôse—Leave this village to go to the village of Herrlisheim, on the road to Lauterbourg. I will notice that it was the 1st *Pluviose* that our meat was taken from us, although we had six *decades (decade was a 10 day week in French Republican Calendar)* of arrears, but it did not last long because we soon returned to the countryside.

11 Pluviôse—Left Herrlisheim to go to Strasbourg. The day after our arrival, General Schauenbourg assembled the officers and non-commissioned officers of several demi-brigades, and made us carry out the great manoeuvre.

13th—Orders came to march towards Switzerland; we left immediately; we stayed in Hüttenheim, near Benfeld; on the 15th in Schlestadt; the 16th in Oberhergheim, a village between Colmar and Ensisheim; the 17th at Baldersheim, a league and a half to the right of Ensisheim, on the road to Basle. The 18th at Rantzwiller, behind and near Sierentz, in the Altkirch valley; on the 19th in Suënaï (?) village in the hill of Mont Terrible, three leagues from Reinach, on the right, and four leagues from Delémont; the 20th at Viques in the Delemont plain; the 21st at Eschert, a small hamlet located three leagues from Delemont, and half a league from Moutier. To get to this hill, we crossed two leagues of rocky mountains as far as the eye could see.

These places are inhabited and form several small towns. This valley had been given freedom a few months before the French were stationed there, they were formerly allied with the Swiss; they close the border of the canton of Solothurn. This valley also belonged to the Prince of Porontruy; who speaks a *patois* that we understand enough.

Their houses are all built of wood, for the most part; all their commerce is in oxen, cows, horses; they have very little arable land. As the hamlets were not very large, they housed a company.

We left Eschert on 3rd *Ventôse* to go to Moutier, capital of the canton and part of the Mont-Terrible department; part of our company was posted to Belpraon, a hamlet near these cantonments. On the 5th, at eight o'clock in the morning, we went to stay in Soncelboz, a village where we had great difficulty in arriving, because snow had been falling for three days, and on that day it had fallen all day, so we had it up to our knees. In the same village, it had been two years in a row that hail had ravaged everything.

8th—Left to go to La Hutte, (all these villages are in the same valley, on the road to Bienne.) Going to La Hutte, we passed under La Roche-Percée. La Hutte was the place where our demi-brigade

94

gathered before going to attack the Swiss. The valley we were leaving was called the Erguel; our column bore its name until the moment it entered Switzerland.

Leaving La Hutte on the 9th at five o'clock in the evening, we followed the road to Biel. We camped three leagues to the left of Bienne, between the road to Bienne and Soleure and to the left of the river called the Aar, half a gunshot from the village of Lengnau where the Swiss outposts were. Measures were taken to attack the Swiss at three o'clock in the morning on 10th *Ventôse*; but the attack did not take place. The Swiss generals made a request to General Schauenbourg, who was in command of the French Army in Switzerland, to grant them a suspension of attack for twenty-four hours, and it lasted until the 12th, which day they were attacked.

12 Ventôse—The attack began at four in the morning; their outposts, which were established in the village of Lengnau, have been removed. The army, which was in the canton, could not resist the ardour of the republican column: their artillery was removed at first sight; because the attack was sharp on our part. In this fight, many Swiss lost their lives, and most of them were fathers: those I spoke to, who had only shattered thighs or legs, missed the wives and children they had left in their homes to come and expose their lives on the borders.

Our camp was three leagues from the capital of this canton, which is Solothurn. Although fortified, it was forced to surrender when our column arrived, without firing a cannon, although its ramparts were well furnished. We entered Solothurn between ten and eleven in the morning, on 12th *Ventôse*. We remained two battalions of our demi-brigade while our column marched. The first evening we were bivouacked on the ramparts until the next day at four o'clock in the evening, when we returned to our accommodation with the *bourgeois*. We couldn't be better received there. Our third battalion was encamped on the road to Lucerne, near a village, within cannon range of the city, while the column was marching on Berne.

Being in the city of Solothurn, General Schauenbourg had to give up arms to all the citizens of the city and to all the inhabitants of this canton. Every day there were cars loaded with guns, cartridge bags and all kinds of weapons, which were placed in the arsenal to be immediately sent to France.

One found in this city an arsenal rather well furnished with various weapons, a quantity of guns in bronze which had been cast in

Strasbourg; a lot of fine powder of two qualities. This city is quite big, there are beautiful streets, but there are several heights which detract from their beauty. It contains many merchants of all kinds. The construction of the houses is very beautiful and quite high.

I noticed in the square where we planted the tree of liberty, a clock whose dial bore the twelve months of the year, and the signs of each. When they arrived, the key landed on it, and there was another small dial that marked the hours. As the hammer struck, there was Death holding a lamp in her left hand, she spun around and likewise shook her head. On the other side, there was a sort of man, who had repentance, because with each blow that the hammer struck, he struck a blow on his chest with his right hand. He was a warrior, for he had the sabre. Beside, between the two, was an old man with a large black beard; he opened his mouth with each blow; and held in his left hand the royal staff, which it swung in all directions.

The Aar River passes Solothurn, and divides it into two unequal parts.

We took a battalion out of town. As it was not large enough to contain two battalions, our battalion was quartered around the city, in the villages. It was on 20 *Ventôse* that each company went to take their designated cantonments, but always in the same canton. I will only name the places where I have been.

Our company was stationed at Subingen, a village a league and a half from Solothurn, on the road which leads from Solothurn to Lucerne, on the other side of the Aare. We changed cantonments several times, in the same canton. Left Subingen on 2nd *Germinal* to stay in the village of Aschi (?) and two and a quarter leagues from Solothurn.

8th Germinal.—We left to go and settle in Langenthal, a town located half a league from the borders of the canton of Lucerne and ten leagues from Bern. I went to see a convent of Bernardins which was on the borders of the canton of Lucerne, where I spoke a little about the convent of Clairvaux; he was of the same order of Citeaux.

Being in this cantonment, we went to Solothurn to carry out the fire exercise. We slept on the 29th, on our way there, in Nider-Bipp, a village in the canton of Bern, on the road to Basel.

30th Germinal—We went to Solothurn; there we did the fire drill for three hours; we were five battalions, artillery and cavalry; it was General Schauenbourg who was in command. After the exercise ended, everyone willingly returned to their cantonments.

6th Floréal—Leaving Langenthal at six o'clock in the morning to go to Zurich, we stayed on our way at Olten, a town in the canton of Solothurn, on the Aare, where there are various routes to Basel, Zurich, etc. I will say that when we entered this canton, the Swiss had burned a superb bridge which crossed the Aare to enter the town of Halte; we were restoring it when we stayed there.

7th Floréal—Leaving Olten at five in the morning, our quarter-masters were as usual to prepare our lodgings. When they presented themselves to the village designated to house four companies, we were there under arms and we told our quartermasters to return, that peace was not made with them, and that they would not did not want to house us.

It was in the village of Bagglingen, we met our quarterbacks who told us that if we wanted to be accommodated, we had to reach the villages. Immediately, the most senior officer of the four companies, arranged the troop to enter the villages. We sent them to ask if they wanted to accommodate us: they answered no and that we withdraw, or that they were going to fire. At that moment, skirmishers were sent and immediately the fire started; they saw us few people and believed that we would soon be defeated, but they were much deceived, because we drove them from their villages, and they largely took refuge in the woods. There were several who had hidden their weapons and were in front of us; they were sent back to their homes. The women fled with their little children to the cradle; all this made pity on the human heart; but also, all those that we caught, we made them return to their homes. Most had a gun in one hand and a rosary in the other.

When they were pushed out of their villages, we returned to take a position behind. Perhaps an hour later, a column of about fifteen hundred men came with two pieces of cannon, and fired two shots which had no effect. We also received reinforcements, light infantry and a detachment of hussars. Gathered together at the beginning of the night, we routed them and we were masters of our cantonments, where we bivouacked.

This village of Bagglingen is in the bailiwick formerly called *Canton-libre-inférieur*. We left on the 9th, at eight o'clock in the morning, to go to Zurich, where we arrived the same day. This city bears the name of the canton where it is located, on the end of the lake of the same name, and from this lake issues a river which passes through Zurich, and is called Limmat, and makes a junction with two other rivers which are called, one the Reuss, which leaves the canton of Lucerne, and the other the Aar, which leaves the canton of Bern. These three rivers are united near a small town called Brugg, and from there fall into the Rhine.

11th Floréal—Departed from Zurich at noon, we went to stay in the village called Thalwyl, located on the lake and two leagues from the city, on the right.

★★★★★★

An entry of French troops into Zurich had been preceded by a proc-lamation which promised that nothing would be asked for the upkeep of the troops, whose pay and subsidies were, it said, provided by con-voys from France. Once in town, however, it was necessary to make requests for food; they were justified by the excuse that the convoys were unfortunately late; a promise was made to return them in kind, on arrival of the convoys, or to reimburse them with the first funds that the Directory would send. The Executive Board agent confirmed this commitment by his presence. A few days later, a decree imposes on the city of Zurich an extraordinary contribution of war payable within a very short time: the abuse of force was the only reason to give for such a lack of faith. A deputation of notables goes to the com-manding general to make representations to him. The general was all the more embarrassed to answer because he himself was not guilty; he had only acted on orders. He was trying, like the first time, to find excuses in the delay of the convoys expected from France, in the pressing needs of the army, when the orator of the deputation relieved him of his embarrassment:

"General," he said to him. "we have not come to reproach you for having forgotten your commitments that you have no doubt been forced to violate, nor to complain that the contribution is too high, but to tell you, on the contrary, *that we can pay more, and beg you to ask us.*"

Then, seizing his hand eagerly: "*When you have taken from us,*" he add-ed, "*riches which have hardened your courage and which our ancestors knew how to do without, we will come back worthy of them, we will come back Swiss .*"

We give according to the *Memoirs* of Marshal Soult (as always) this beautiful feature which is to be meditated at all times and in all coun-tries.

★★★★★★

12th—At two o'clock in the morning, we went to camp near the village called Lachen and similarly located on the lake in the canton of Schwyz.

13th—Left at nine in the morning to retrace our steps and stay in the village of Frienbach; there were four of us, the same companies that had been in Bagglingen. This village and the others that have been named are on the lake to the right. Leaving Zurich, we were not as soon as we arrived in the cantonment, that an attack formed between the Swiss of the canton of Schwyz and some companies of the 76th Line Demi-Brigade, around eleven o'clock in the morning.

At the same time, Citizen Mondragon, who was the oldest in rank of the captains of the detachment, immediately gave orders to beat the double blows, to assemble the companies and to march towards the place of the attack. Instead of going where we were fighting, said captain made us climb a stupendous mountain, to take them from behind. In fact, the mountain was crossed with great courage; at the top, the troop commander made the charge beat. Before we were at the top of the mountain, we were already assailed by gunshots.

While the charge was fighting, we started firing on the Swiss, who came to dispute the ground with us; but they had to give in, or they would have paid for everything. In this affair, several fathers of families remained on the battlefield; afterwards, the highest mountains no longer reassured them, they abandoned their cottages and went to retire in uninhabitable places. The same day, at sunset, we went down the mountain and returned to our cantonment.

14th—Left at two o'clock in the morning, to prepare us for new pursuits. We took the road which leads to Notre-Dame-des-Hermites; we climbed a very high mountain, and, being at the top, near a large inn, we occupied the position which the Swiss had abandoned the day before. This mountain is called Etzel, and is a league from the convent of Notre-Dame-des-Hermites, where it is easily seen. In the vicinity of this convent, no grain is harvested; it is also surrounded by mountains covered with snow. In this region, there are pastures for the horned animals; so that's what feeds them: a few potatoes, cheese and milk.

16th—We returned to the cantonments of the 13th.

21st—Leaving Frienbach at eight o'clock in the morning, our march was directed to the Ligurian Republic in Italy. I will say that we passed to the town named Rapperswyl, located on the lake, on the left side. Before entering the city, there is a bridge that is half a league, (It is 1,800 feet long. I will only name the places where we stayed; for the journey is so long and the time so short that I cannot make many observations.

21st Floréal.—Arrived at the village called Thatwyl, at daybreak, we left on the 22nd at eight o'clock in the morning; we passed Zurich at ten o'clock; we continued our journey crossing several high mountains and came to stay in the vicinity of Mellingen, a village located on the Reuss in the village where we were; this village was called Waltenschwyl.

23rd—Leaving this village at six in the morning, we came to stay in Aarburg, in the canton of Bern, located on the Aare, where there is a fairly large fort.

24th—Left at seven in the morning, we came to stay in the vicinity of Herzogenbachsee; we were at Niederhaus; our company also in the canton of Bern.

25th—Left at five in the morning. Housed in the city of Bern. I noticed that there was a nice big street; that it goes a little uphill, and at the distance of eighty feet there is a fountain. I saw a rather curious clock: all the time that the hammer strikes on the bell, there is a tower near the dial, made like a round table on which there are bears parading in parade, with instruments of war; there are some who are mounted on horses: well, that is amusing.

All the streets of this city are adorned with beautiful arcades where there are all kinds of merchants. Above the door, on the Lausanne side, the person of Guillaume (*William*) Tell is represented.

27th Floréal.—Left at four in the morning. Lodged in Morat town located on the lake of that name.

28th—Left at six in the morning. Lodged around Payerne; we were in the village of Fétigny.

29th—Left at three in the morning. Lodged in Moudon in the country of Vaux, formerly allied with Bern, and located on the edge of the Broye. This city was formerly the capital of the country; we can still see today an old tower which was built in the time of Julius Caesar.

30th—Left at four in the morning, we came to stay in Lausanne, the capital of its canton, located at the foot of a mountain, on the shores of Lake Geneva. All of the places we've been are largely vineyards.

1st Prairial—Left at three in the morning, we followed the lake, and came to stay in Villeneuve and the surrounding area. This city is located on the end of Lake Geneva; our company was lodged in a village a league from Villeneuve, and between extremely high mountains, where there is always a quantity of snow at the top.

3rd—Left at eight o'clock in the morning, we came to stay in Saint-Maurice, in the lower Valais. Before entering the city, we cross a bridge that crosses the Rhône and will fall into Lake Geneva.

4th—Left at six in the morning. Stayed in Orsières in the lower Valais, on the road that leads to the great Saint-Bernard.

5th—Left Orsières at seven in the morning. Lying in Saint-Pierre, a village on the path that leads to Mont Saint-Bernard; it is from this village that the road forms only a very bad path for walking; wagons can no longer pass there unless they are dismantled and carried by mules ten leagues away, where the city of Aoste is.

All the places we have been since Villeneuve are located between large and very high mountains, at the top covered with snow; but still the hill is cultivated. I noticed that two leagues from Saint-Maurice there are very high rocks; at a hundred feet high, it comes out of the water in quantity; seeing it fall it appears white as milk, it breaks on stones which are at the bottom of this rock and passes in the path as clear as crystal. This place is called the Pisse-vache.

6th—Left Saint-Pierre, the last village in the lower Valais, at two in the morning to go up to the village of the mountain of Saint-Bernard which goes up for three hours, and goes down as much; in this mountain there is more snow than in the others. We went through places (and especially before we were at the convent) where there were more than forty feet, but it was all frozen snow. Arriving near the convent, we climbed on all fours on the snow; it is really terrible roads; so many travellers die on the way.

The convent, which is at the top of this mountain, is there to give assistance to travellers; there are dogs that I have seen; they are extremely strong and educated. When there are thunderstorms or bad weather, these dogs go through the snow on the path; they have a cloth around their necks in which there is a small bottle of brandy with a piece of bread; if they meet someone who has fallen weak or has lost heart and is seized by the cold, whether on a rock or elsewhere, these dogs go near, take him by his clothing and move him ;

and if he is not dead, they present his neck to him so that he can take what is in the linen to give him strength. Sometimes they find some lying in the snow, and as there are servants who follow them from afar, they return to them and lead them where the men have fallen.

Being in the convent, one can stay there one day; all the troop which passed there received by man a glass of wine, a small piece of bread and also salted meat. We continued on the road, because we would have frozen well if we had stayed there for a quarter of an hour; finally, in the vicinity of this convent, there are real precipices. Our path was marked with pieces of wood, otherwise there would have been some of us who would have lost their lives.

That day, we came to stay in Saint-Oyen, a village on the road to Sardinia. In these villages, and even before climbing the Saint-Bernard, the inhabitants cook only once a year; if they cook twice, it is because they are very comfortable; their bread is an inch and a foot thick and hard as wood; much of their food is milk and potatoes.

7th—Leaving Saint-Oyen at five in the morning, we came to stay in the city of Aoste, city of Sardinia, border of Savoy and Switzerland.

9th—Leaving Aoste at two in the morning, we came to stay in Verres, a town in the Aoste Valley and likewise in Sardinia.

10th—Left from Verres at three in the morning. Lodged in Ivrée, on the River Doire, in Piedmont.

11th—Left at four in the morning. Lodged in Livorno.

12th—Left at four in the morning. Lodged in Verceil, on the River Sesia.

13th—Left at six in the morning. Lodged at Gailliata, eight leagues from Milan, and one league from Trecate.

15th—Left at two in the morning. Lodged in Vigevano, on the road to Alexandria.

16th—Left at midnight, we crossed the Po at noon, and we came to stay in Voghera.

17th—Left at two in the morning. Lodged in Alexandria, a strong city held hostage to the French when the King of Sardinia made peace; this city is located on the Tanaro River which passes between the citadel and the walls of this city.

19th—Left Alexandria at ten in the morning. Lodged in Novi, a town in Piedmont, on the border of the Ligurian Republic.

20th—Left at three in the morning. At seven o'clock we passed at the bottom of Gavi Fort, where we stopped. We passed in the midst of the Genoese and Piedmontese Army which was encamped in the vicinity of Fort Gavi. In this time, the Ligurians had war with Piedmont. The same day, camped near Voltagio, on the road to Genoa.

21st—Left the camp at three in the morning. Camped two leagues from Genoa. It is from there that our first battalion left to go to Genoa, and our third retraced its steps to go to Novi; we slept in this village.

22nd—Left at three in the morning to return to the borders of the Ligurian Republic; we stayed that day at Voltagio.

23rd—Leaving at two o'clock in the morning, we took the crossing and went to stay in Ovada, a border town of the Ligurian Republic, threatened by Piedmontese troops of being looted. That is why our battalion went to seize the city to save it from such a misfortune; this city is surrounded by two rivers which are called Stura and Orba. While we were in this town, we were detained twenty-six non-commissioned officers in prison for making a claim; we have been twelve days in *the shade*. (*In the army, the prison is so named because it is not allowed to enter the daylight.*)

19th Messidor—Left for Camfredo, town of Liguria.

20th—Left at one in the morning. Lodged in Voltri, eight and a half leagues from Genoa.

23rd—Lodged in Varazze, also on the sea.

24th—Lodged in Savona, where there is a commercial port; there is also a fort which defends its approach well and can beat the city.

25th—Lodged in Final-Borgo.

26th—Left at two in the morning. Lodged in Albenga. All the places where we stayed are located on the sea.

28th—Left at one o'clock in the morning for a small town called La Piève, located in the same valley and six leagues from the sea. At La Piève, we found the Piedmontese garrison which had seized this town at the time when they were united in the war. France ended this war, which could only put famine in the country.

As this country resembles most of the Ligurian Republic of which it is a part, I will give a small description of the situation of country. They are only very high mountains, most of them covered with chestnut trees, olive trees, fig trees and other fruit trees of all kinds of species; there is also very light and tall vine planted, among which they sow wheat and other grains, which they use to make bread; but these do not are not very abundant there. All this country is occupied largely by the trade which is good there, compared to the sea.

There is nothing curious to see in the countryside; their houses are very ancient and all vaulted, to ward off the heat which occurs in this country during the summer. There is nothing remarkable about their households, most of them have no furniture, only a chest to put what little clothing they have. The interiors of the houses are very dark and most of them do not have windows; a simple shutter closes the day. You can hardly see any chimneys there: they make a fire in one of the corners of the house. Both sexes are dressed quite antiquated; women and girls wear a large veil on their heads to go to church. These people are inherently traitorous, they have always hidden under them a very sharp and cutting weapon, and at the slightest difficulty one is struck by this tool.

8th Frimaire—Left from La Pième for Genoa, we went to lodge in Loano; on the 9th, in Varazze; the 10th, in Genoa. Being in this city we provided a detachment of three hundred men to go and seize the city of Oneglia, belonging to Piedmont. The Piedmontese garrison was disarmed and sent to Genoa, but their arms were immediately sent to them to leave for the borders of Italy. This was done at the time of the Piedmont revolution. The detachment of which I was part left Genoa on 20 *Frimaire*, at one in the afternoon; we stayed on our way to Oneglia, Voltri, Savona, Finalborgo and Alassio. There were three hundred Ligurians with us. This city surrendered to our approach; we entered it on 24 *Frimaire* at four in the evening. The rest of our battalion, which was in Genoa, came to join us on 15 *Nivôse*; There were only two companies left in Oneglia, and the others pressed to the left along the sea. This movement took place on the 15th.

Our company was in Diano-Marino and Alassio. Leaving these cantonments on the 1st *Pluviôse*, we came to Genoa on the 5th, where our demi-brigade met to form two war battalions and one for peace. The latter was made up of helpless, crippled men who could no longer campaign and supplemented with conscripts. The two war battalions were made up of seasoned men and able to campaign with about twenty of the most skilful conscripts per company, drawn from the third battalion. In this amalgamation, we became the third company of the first battalion. This enrolment took place in Genoa on 8th *Pluviôse*. The first battalion left from Genoa on the 9th to go to Reggio; the second battalion on the 10th, for the same route. I was not in this departure, I entered the hospital on the 10th; I had an illness that prevented me from marching.

20th Ventôse—Left the city of Genoa to go to Reggio. When leaving the country of Liguria, I left a country quite abundant in olive and chestnut trees; they also collect a certain quantity of wine and grains; the greatest occupation of the inhabitants is commerce. They breed a quantity of silkworms nourished by the mulberry trees which grow in this country. Here I entered Piedmont while leaving Novi; I lodged on the 23rd at Tortone, a fortified town accompanied by a fairly considerable fort, on a height which commands the town; on the 24th, in Voghera; the 25th, in Castel-San-Giovani, a town dependent on the King of Spain; on the 26th, at Plaisance, a beautiful large city owned by the King of Spain, magnificently built. There is a superb place there on which are placed two pedestals on which are two bronze horses with their warriors. It is very well decorated with beautiful houses; the streets are very wide and well proportioned. Formerly, this city was fortified, but there are only old ramparts that are falling into ruins.

27th—Lodged in Borgo-San-Domino, likewise in the States of the King of Spain.

28th—In Parma, belonging to the duchy of its name; the river of the same name, Parma, passes through the said town and divides it into two unequal parts; the construction is quite beautiful, the streets wide, there are also quite pretty squares.

29th—In Reggio, a large and well-populated city, now in the Cisalpine Republic; there is a beautiful square, very wide streets; it was once fortified, now there is still an old citadel which is falling into ruins and which could not last long. I had stay in this city.

1st Germinal—In Modena; the city is longer than it is wide: the streets are wide, the houses fairly high and beautifully constructed; there are beautiful large squares. This city is still a little fortified.

3rd—In Buondeno, a village near Ferrara.

4th—In Finale, a town on the canal from the city of Modena.

5th—At La Mirandole, a fairly well-built small town where there is a beautiful square.

6th—In Saint-Benedetto, a village five leagues from Mantua.

7th—In Mantua, a beautiful large city with a large population; it is surrounded by large parts of water which defend its approach of half a league; on the side where the water is not so wide, there are strong citadels which defend the city; the surroundings of this place, as well as the forts, are lined with many large cannons which make this city impregnable, other than by famine. The river called Po passes through its walls, and gives it a quantity of water; the construction of the houses is beautiful, there are beautiful places. I saw there a beautiful covered bridge built entirely in freestone; there are seven to eight very well-built mills on this bridge. This place belongs to the Cisalpine Republic; it was taken by the French who were commanded by Bonaparte.

On the 8th, I passed through Villefranche, on the road to Verona, where I found our battalion, which was encamped two and a half leagues from the town, near the road. They had come there after the affair of 6th *Germinal*, on which day this terrible scourge of war rekindled with the emperor. Our division, commanded by Montrichard, made its attack near the village of Legnago, located on the Adige.

The attack was sharp at first on our part: it seemed before noon that the victory was announced to us; but, as fate does not decide in an instant, we saw, around three in the evening, that we had had to deal with an Austrian Army corps which equalled our own. In the evening, a reinforcement arrived to them; it is to the latter, united to the former, that we had to give up the victory which had been favourable to us all day. Many ditches filled with water caused us some losses. I will not say the losses of the other corps, I saw those of my battalion which amounted to 148 men *hors de combat,* including ten officers and ten non-commissioned officers. While waiting for the siege, we made several movements to the right and to the left along the Adige, where the Austrian Army corps was well entrenched.

Here is *Germinal* 16th arrived. Towards ten o'clock in the morning the enemy set out to attack us; the general-in-chief gave orders to all our troops to march in order to attack the enemy in the same way, which was carried out on the spot.

★★★★★★

Germinal 16th corresponds to April 5th, 1799. Marshal Soult sums up this series of setbacks due to the incapacity of General Scherer as follows: "General Scherer left from the places of Mantua and Peschiera, on the Mincio line: he began his operations. March 26th, to force the line of the Adige. It operated with three columns: the one on the left, commanded by General Moreau, was advancing. It passed the Adige over Verona, cutting off the right of the Austrian Army, and it was in a position to continue its successes towards Vienna if it had been supported; but the other divisions of the centre and the right, which General Scherer commanded in person, were beaten by the enemy.

However, the success that General Moreau had just won was enough for the rest of the army to be able to rely on him, to join him, marching on Vienna, throwing the Austrians back on the Brenta and separating them from the places of Verona and Legnago. General Moreau gave this advice to General Scherer; but, instead of following him, the latter had the singular idea of recalling General Moreau to the right bank of the Adige, to recommence the same operation on his right, four days later. This time the lesson was more severe: part of Serurier's division was lost there, compromised by a night of false movements on the left bank of the Adige, and which, surrounded by superior forces, ended up being overwhelmed.

"Finally, a third attempt, made on April 6th, was even less successful. In spite of successes, first gained in the centre by General Moreau, the right of the army was turned, at the end of the day, by a skilful manoeuvre of General Kray. There was so much inconsistency in all the movements that this failure could not be repaired: disorder joined in and the entire army precipitated its retreat, not only behind the Mincio where General Scherer could have held, in support of the places of Peschiera and Mantua, but behind the Adda.

"Magnano's day decided the fate of Italy. Ten days had sufficed to reduce the army to less than thirty thousand combatants, while on the other hand, all the troops scattered from the Po to Naples, were not only too far away to bring reinforcements to it in time, but day by day they found themselves more compromised. At the same time, the enemy army had replaced all its losses and it was acquiring greater and greater superiority through the reinforcements it received at all times; it was, moreover, on the eve of being joined by the Russian Army, which arrived on the Adige on April 15th.

"The exasperation of the army, whose courage had been so badly employed, was at its height, and it would have produced acts of indiscipline and disobedience, if General Scherer had remained. He understood this, he left for Milan on the pretext of directing the extraordinary levies that were being carried out there, and did not return. He had handed over command to General Moreau before his departure."

★★★★★★

We immediately encountered the Austrian columns; the fire was alive in both parties; at first glance it seemed that our division was about to yield to the strength of the Austrian column.

The soldier did not measure his strength on those of his enemy, but on his courage: he routed the enemy column, taking a few hundred prisoners. We pursued them to the gates of Verona; but the retreat of the other divisions soon taught us that we should also dispose of ourselves there during the night, and withdraw to the environs of Mantua, which was done on the night of the 16th to the 17th, because a considerable body of the Austrian Army was advancing to cut off our retreat beyond Mantua.

We arrived seven miles from Mantua around midnight, on the night of the 17th to the 18th. On the crossing of the road which leads to Villefranche, on the 18th, we made a movement to press to the left of Mantua. We came to camp near a small town on the Mincio; it was surrounded by strong positions. When the garrison of Mantua was established in its posts, the army set in motion and crossed the Mincio to go and show itself in the plain where Bonaparte had great battles, when it was necessary to surround the city of Mantua. We stayed in this plain, which ends on the bank of the Mincio, until eight in the evening. It was the night of the 20th to the 21st that our column began its movement for the retreat, the evening of the 21st around six o'clock, in abominable weather, a continual rain which did not stop falling and chilled us to the bones. We camped near the small town of Asola; its surroundings are lined with bastions which were not well maintained.

22nd Germinal—Camped three thousand near to Pontevico; on the 24th, we came to camp in front of this small town, located on the edge of the river called Oglio, on the road to Brescia and Milan. At that moment we were in the rear; we cut the roads to prevent the Austrian column from pursuing us so closely.

25th—We passed the Oglio on a drawbridge which was at the bottom of an old citadel: the troops and the baggage passed, we dismantled the bridge by sliding it into the water. That day we came to the village of Rodierco, located on the Oglio and one mile from Pontevico, on the main road to Milan. The night of the 25th to the 26th, we set off and we arrived at Palazzolo on the evening of the 26th. It should be noted that the Austrian column took detours and followed the mountains of Italian Switzerland and sought only to cut off our retreat.

28th—We made a movement in front of Palazzolo, six thousand in the mountains, near Lake Iseo.

29th—We returned to Palazzolo; on the 30th, we left to form ourselves on the line in battle, in front of the said place. General-in-Chief Scherer reviewed us. We spent the night in this same location. The Town of Palazzolo is located on the Oglio and on the main road to Brescia. On leaving, the bridges were cut and overturned in the river.

2nd Floréal—We made a movement to retire behind Palazzolo, where we camped, on the banks of the Oglio; our outposts had some small business with the enemy, who came forward to cross the bridge where our gunners were, to blow it up with mines; we managed to blow it up around ten in the morning.

On the night of the 4th to the 5th, at nine o'clock in the evening, our division, which was that of General Serrurier, set out and was directed towards the city of Bergamo. We spent a dreadful night in water and mud up to our knees, and, to make it complete, a continual rain showered us. We passed through the town of Bergamo at eleven o'clock in the morning on the 3rd. This town is very large, beautiful and rich: a very fine plaza was being built there; it is divided into upper town and lower town. The upper town is fortified and has very beautiful positions in its surroundings, on considerable heights. Our division did not stop there; part supported the rear guard, which was attending to Russian troops. (The Russian Army had joined forces.) The same day, our column continued its march until five in the evening; we arrived at the edge of the lake, where we spent the night in a sort of small hamlets surrounded by very high mountains.

The next day, at four o'clock in the morning, we resumed our march towards the Lecco bridge, and still closely followed by the enemy vanguard. The town of Lecco is surrounded by very high rocks; it is located on the edge of the lake. Our division crossed the bridge the day the enemy arrived. A part of our division kept the head of the bridge, and the other part extended on the banks of the river, to correspond with the division of General Delmas; our battalion was of this part; we were at that moment on the right of the division. We came to take our position, the night of the 6th to the 7th, at Vaprio, where we arrived at eleven o'clock in the morning. This town is located on the edge of the river called the Adda; it is strong by its position: there was an established flying bridge that we sank when we left the river.

At about two o'clock in the afternoon, a sizable column of the

Austrian Army made a movement to prepare to cross the river during the night, which was easy for them, for the river was hardly guarded. Around four in the morning, as our battalion was bivouacking in a village a league and a half from Vaprio, an ordinance came to tell the general who commanded this post that the Austrian Army had crossed the river, all night and directed his march on Milan.

★★★★★★

This is the passage of the Adda on the right of Berthier's army which had moved towards the eastern point of Lake Como, and which isolated the Serrurier division from the rest of the army. The general attack of the enemy triumphed on the other points, and the French Army saw itself reduced to the retreat after having lost the third of its force and a hundred guns.

★★★★★★

We were immediately ordered to retreat to Vaprio, to join General Delmas' division, leaving companies in echelons at intervals; until we found a route from Vaprio to Milan, which was already cut off by the enemy. The fight immediately began on the left bank of the Adda, in the vicinity of Vaprio and Casale; which was stubborn on both sides. General Delmas came to order the battalions which were supporting the attack, which were ours and one of the 3rd Demi-Brigade, to rush on the enemy, and he said that his division would arrive to support us.

As soon as the order was given, the two battalions set out for the execution; in an instant victory smiled upon us, making about two hundred men prisoners; but at the same time, a considerable reinforcement having arrived, they forced the battalion which was on our right, on the bank of the river, and they were not long in taking ours by the flank and the front. In these hotter than usual disputes, I received a bullet which crossed my left forearm and put me out of action, from which I escaped with great difficulty, because we were taken from all sides.

But the division arrived at this moment and gave us a break; the day had become terrible for both parties. When Delmas' division engaged, it pushed back the enemy at the head of the bridge; there was a village where the enemy was entrenched within the garden walls and our people were all around; the enemy seeing that he could not shoot anymore because of the height of the walls, took the stones of the walls to throw them on the heads of the French, but the republican ardour which boiled in the veins of the soldiers, did not suffer long the insult of the Germans; As soon as they entered the village with the bayonet forward, they overthrew a large number of them and took seven hundred prisoners. The streets of the village were watered that day with the blood of the Germans, because blood flowed in the streets.

The fight did not cease until night stretched its veils in the surroundings where it had started. But we retreated to Milan; the town of Casale is still seven leagues from it and some of the wounded have been forced to follow the column; the roads were intercepted. We arrived around midnight in Milan, from the 8th to the 9th. The column passed through Milan between eight and nine in the morning, on the 9th. Although our wounds were not healed and the march made us suffer we had preferred to follow our column which came to the edges of the Ticino than to see us taken prisoner by inhuman troops. Only the troops remained at the castle of Milan.

It was on the banks of the Ticino that I left my companions in misery with regret, but my injury demanded it. On leaving, after three battles, I left a quartermaster, a corporal and six fusiliers, in a company which was, on 6th *Germinal*, made up of one hundred and ten men.

Our Army of Mantua was obliged, by a superior force of enemies, to evacuate this part of Italy, and to withdraw to the fortified towns of Piedmont. The hospitals were no longer large enough to contain all the wounded, so it was therefore necessary to return to France.

Before leaving this part of Italy, I want to give a little description of the situation of the inhabitants and of the fertility of the land in this region. From Mont-Cenis in Mantua, it is flat and sandy terrain; it is planted with all kinds of trees, but it is the mulberry trees that dominate; the vine is very common there and is planted at the foot of all these trees: it produces excellent wines; one sees there in no country the vines attached to the top of very large trees, and this vine yields a considerable quantity of grapes. The inhabitants of the country cut the branches of these trees every year to cook their food.

They sow grains of all kinds of species under these vines, which still do quite well there compared to the trees and vines which give them freshness, otherwise they could not harvest anything because of the great heat of the country. In Piedmont and other regions, they sow a lot of rice which forms part of their food only with vermicelli; finally, they hardly eat anything except pasta. The occupation of these inhabitants is largely trade, and the breeding of silkworms which gives them a large number of manufactures. There are, in this part of Italy, fairly beautiful sexes on both sides, but extremely jealous and treacherous. There are also strong rivers and mediocre ones that water the rice plains. The construction of the houses is quite pleasant.

In this region are locked up several small states and republics, which means that there are several currencies, but which are not worth that of France, except that of Piedmont which is better. Formerly, this country was very rich, but it had to deal with several masters who took away all its wealth, and the war ended its ruin. I will not make much observation on the places where I passed, having evacuated from Milan to Dijon.

On 5th *Prairial*, we arrived in Dijon, the destination for the wounded; we entered the military hospital, all newly prepared to receive the wounded who arrived in large numbers every day.

I stayed eleven days at this Dijon hospital, where my wound was dressed twice a day. During this time, I made several requests to the health officers for convalescence. As I was only twenty-four hours from my home and it was seven years since I had returned home, I saw myself having a little hope of seeing my father again and mother, as well as my grandparents. I received from the health officers of the military hospital of Dijon, a convalescence furlough of twenty days to go and heal my wound in my home; it was delivered to me on 16h *Prairial*. I went to Longchamp on the 19th *via* Langres; from there I took the crossing to turn off as short as possible. So, I arrived the day before the feast that was being celebrated for the plenipotentiaries who had been slaughtered in Rastadt.

The commissioner of the executive power and the president did me the honour of putting on the ceremony; they did me the honours by sending for me by a detachment of the National Guard; I was immediately offered a place of honour which was next to the president, which I accepted. After the ceremony, I was admitted to the meal that the administrators gave themselves. I was received with all the pomp and honour due to a defender of his country who had never given up his flag.

My convalescence having expired and not being in a condition to go and rejoin, I went to see the canton health officer; not finding my arm well enough restored, he gave me a period of six *decades* (*i.e.,* sixty days in French Republican calendar), which were over on the 30th of *Fructidor*, I asked for my road map to go and join my unit and share with my old comrades, the honour that I've already shared the space of seven years. I hope that the Supreme Being will bless our work for the salvation of the whole of France. (As a complement to this invocation, see the prayer at the end of the journal.)

I left Longchamp on the 1st *Vendémiaire* year VIII of the Republic, to join my corps on the borders of Italy.

My departure was delayed for a month at Chaumont where I stayed to teach the exercise to a company of conscripts from this department. After the organisation of this battalion, I resumed my journey for the Italian border. I left Chaumont on 16th *Brumaire* of the year VIII, accompanied by my young brother who had left the 9th *Chasseurs à Cheval*, to come and take service in the 3rd line Demi-Brigade which was currently in Italy. We drove quite pleasantly from Chaumont to Aix en Provence. I will pass over in silence the astonishment of my brother during this journey, to find himself in a country so deserted and so infertile, under the rocks of Provence. I will give a little description.

After having travelled through several regions of Provence, having reached our depot in Aix on 21st *Frimaire*, we were three leagues away, on the Durance, to a village called Peyrolles, until the 1st *Thermidor*. We were there to get the conscripts and requisitioners to join; also, to prevent the assassinations that bands of brigands often carried out in several of these regions; in short, these bands of scoundrels brought desolation to several fathers of families. We left Aix on 5th *Thermidor* to go to another part of Provence, a town called Draguignan, where we arrived on the 9th.

This town is located in the middle of a plain surrounded by high mountains; the country is charming, one sees a prodigious quantity of olive trees there; the slopes which surround the city form an amphitheatre planted with olive trees which form a tapestry, green in winter as in summer, which delights the view, and gives a beautiful view. The plain which surrounds the city is planted with vines between which several kinds of grains and vegetables are sown.

The waters are very good there, the country being watered by fountains coming from the mountains. The city is closed by a simple wall, very high; the streets are of a width proportionate to their length, but very badly maintained as cleanliness: they let rot all kinds of grass coming from the mountains to make fertilizer for the earth. In Provence, there are very few *amenities*, which means that all the garbage is thrown in the streets; this is what makes the country unhealthy; we breathe bad smells. It is reported that they do not give themselves the ease of the *conveniences* because of the quantity of the conduits of their fountains which cross their dwellings. The houses are of a rather beautiful construction, three stories high, more or less; the inhabitants are naturally rude and not very human. (Let them tell each other!) What

113

points out their lack of humanity towards their fellow citizens is that in these regions and even throughout the whole of Provence, there is a real considerable amount of brigands who do not stop murdering travellers on the highways every day. I let myself be told that this had always been done, but not as often as now.

The costume of men is not very different from that of our country: the fashion is to wear almost all jackets; females dress almost alike here, except that their skirts are slit from behind; their character is no better than that of men.

The way I portray the region of Draguignan will serve as a model for all of Provence, more or less fertile in food of all kinds. I remember that the country air is warmer there than in our countries; the harvests are done there earlier than here, but also, they plant all summer because the culture could never feed the population withdrawn in this country. Bread is almost always at four and five cents a four-ounce pound. Wine is cheap there, but storms are frequent; therefore, their cultivated land is often ravaged. The grain they reap, they trample under the feet of mules and oxen to remove the seeds.

The evils that I have endured for eight years of military service for my homeland have been marked day by day by new sacrifices that I cannot forget. These sufferings have been repeated several times. So, I will, in this sheet, sketch a sketch of what happened in Genoa during the blockade. Our enemy, wishing to deprive us of all hope of returning to Italy, has assembled great forces to invest Genoa and lock up our army. After several bloody fights on both sides, and on several occasions our enemy having forced our line on Savona, he cut us off the communication that we still had on land, and the English dominated the sea so we could not without great difficulty pass, we are therefore obliged to withdraw under the city of Genoa, while waiting for some reinforcements which did not arrive soon enough. We must therefore understand the misery that we have suffered in this blockade.

★★★★★★

"The picture of the situation of Genoa in the last days of the siege has already been drawn so many times and has become so famous," said Marshal Soult, "that I can limit myself here to recalling it. The horrors of hunger in a city of 160,000 souls are beyond anything most hideous the imagination can imagine. All the animals had been devoured, including dogs and rats; They made, under the name of bread, a composition of almonds, linseed, bran and cocoa, which has been compared to peat soaked in oil, and which even dogs could not bear; the ration consisted of two ounces of this dreadful mixture.

114

The St. Bernard Pass

"Finally, on 15th *Prairial* (June 4), there was not an ounce left for each; there was nothing left that could be eaten, not even the foulest food. There was no more left for the army than for the inhabitants who died by the hundreds every day. The army, if we could still give it that name, did not number three thousand men able to hold a rifle, for making them make the slightest movement was absolutely impossible; the sentries could only make their faction seated. The next day, they could not have done it, all soldiers and inhabitants, would have died of starvation.

"It was only on that day that General Masséna consented to listen to the proposals which had been made to him for several days by the enemy generals, in the most honourable terms. The conference between General Masséna, Austrian generals Ott and Saint-Julien and Admiral Keith commanding the English squadron, was held in the middle of the Cornigliano bridge, on the Bisague, and General Masséna brought to it all the firmness of his character. He began by not wanting to admit the use of the word *capitulation*, and the only expression to which he consented was that of *negotiating for the evacuation of Genoa*.

"The army left Genoa freely with arms and baggage, to return to France, without committing its word: eight thousand men would take the land road; the surplus, as well as hospitals, equipment and everything belonging to the army, would be transported by sea to Antibes. This clause of the march, by land, of eight thousand men, was on the point of breaking off the negotiations. General Ott did not want to consent, in order to delay the reunion of this column to the French Army. General Masséna broke off the conference: 'See you tomorrow, gentlemen,' he told them. However, he knew full well that he would be incapable of fulfilling his threat. This firmness succeeded, but General Masséna was especially assisted by the pressing orders that General Ott had just received from General Mélas, and who ordered him not to waste a moment in raising the siege and in leading his army corps to Alexandria."

★★★★★★

If the inhabitants of the nation owe recognition to its defenders, they owe it in particular to the troops who made up the garrison of Genoa, either by their sufferings or by their intrepidity in defending the city despite the lack of food. A little bread made with chopped straw, bran, cocoa, a little honey to be able to bind this mixture together; and when it was taken out of the oven did it crumble into dust. The meat was very lean mullet; dogs and cats made our best meals. Thanks to Bacchus juice! otherwise we would all have remained hostage under the walls of Genoa. If the city capitulated, it is the lack of food and the great mortality which was the only cause. At the time of

The French Army crossing the St. Bernard Pass

surrender, we received six ounces of this bad bread-making per man, but always a bottle of wine.

The surrender was honourable for us; we took as much artillery as we could, all our baggage and other armaments; all our sick and wounded were brought to France on English ships.

It was after the famous Battle of Marengo that the French returned to the city of Genoa and that there was a suspension of arms, to come to a conclusion of peace; so that the enemy had the city of Genoa three days in possession, then it was returned by arrangement with six other cities and forts.

At that moment, having returned to Draguignan to our depot, we were sent to Digne, in the Basses-Alpes, to take the thermal waters where I used them without being relieved, so that I was returned to my home on 5th *Vendémiaire*, year IX. I arrived at Longchamp-sur-Laujon on 29th *Vendémiaire*.

PRAYER OF THE REPUBLICAN SOLDIER

N.B This prayer ends the manuscript, it is also from Fricasse's hand. At first glance, it had seemed to us the extract of a constitutional priest's sermon, but we changed our mind when we saw the incorrect turn of certain sentences, lines 16, 17, 23, and especially the last lines.

It could perfectly well be the work of a sergeant, and above all of a sergeant who began in the convent as a gardener. It must be recognised that there is a just and noble thought in the second paragraph.

PRAYER OF THE FRENCH REPUBLICAN SOLDIER

God of all justice, eternal and supreme sovereign, arbiter of the destiny of all men, you who are the author of all good and all justice, could you reject the prayer of the virtuous man who asks you only justice and freedom?

Ah! if our cause is unjust, don't defend it! The prayer of the ungodly is a second sin, it is to outrage yourself to ask yourself what is not in accordance with your holy will.

But we ask that the power with which you have invested us be in accordance with your will.

Take under your holy protection a generous nation which fights only for equality.

Take away from our detestable enemies the criminal force to harm us; break the irons of the proud despots who want to forge them for us.

Bless the flag of union under which we all want to come together to achieve our independence.

Bless the generous citizens who risk their lives and their fortunes to defend their homeland.

Bless the respectable mothers of these virtuous children of the fatherland who ask you to grant them victory.

Open the eyes of those who are lost in our homes so that they may come to their senses, to enjoy with us the precious fruits of equality and freedom, and sing with us the hymns and praises dedicated to the Supreme Being.

We worship God each in our own way, under the protection of the law and under the supervision of established authority, and we are only better Republicans.

Bürgerliche Tracht 1790–1792.

Infanterie 1790.

Grenadier 1794.

Husar 1796.

Linien-Kavallerie 1796.

Infanterie 1796.

General 1795.

Leichte Infanterie Offizier 1795.

Linien-Infanterie 179

CLOTHING AND UNIFORMS OF THE PERIOD

Supplement Extra

RISING IN MASS

The project of rising in mass had made the Convention hesitate at first: it astonished it by its boldness; it referred it to the Committee of Public Safety for examination. It was August 12th. On the 14th, Carnot was added to the committee; on the 16th the decree was issued amidst universal acclamations; on the 23rd, a law organised in these terms the *permanent requisition of all the French for the defence of the fatherland*:

> The young people will go into battle; married men will forge arms and transport provisions; the women will make tents, clothes, and serve in hospitals; children will shed old laundry; the old men will be carried to the public places to excite the courage of the warriors, to preach the hatred of kings and the unity of the Republic;
>
> National houses will be converted into barracks, public places into weapons workshops; the cellar floor will be washed to extract the saltpetre;
>
> The calibre weapons will be exclusively given to those who will march to the enemy: the service of the interior will be done with hunting rifles and knives;
>
> Saddle horses are required to complete the cavalry corps; draft horses and others than those employed in agriculture will drive artillery and provisions.
>
> The Committee of Public Safety is responsible for taking the necessary measures to establish without delay an extraordinary manufacture of weapons of all kinds, which responds to the enthusiasm and energy of the French people

France soon offered her adversaries the picture which Barère had thus drawn up in advance.

At Valmy, at Jemmapes again, the regular army had played the only part; but, dating from the time we are relating, it was absorbed by the multitude of volunteers and requisitioners. Henceforth the Republic will be served less on the battlefields by professional soldiers than by citizens destined to quit the uniform after the completion of their crusade: a great example which revealed to the French their aptitude for quickly acquiring the qualities of the soldier. It is not that, in the first moments, these conscripts who did not know how to hold their weapon, who rushed madly and disbanded at the slightest shock, did not give tablature to the generals; the correspondence of representatives is strewn with complaints and concerns about them; but their novitiate was not long. Jomini said:

> From the end of August, the effects of the new levy were felt; the unblocking of Dunkirk and that of Maubeuge were the first results, and the great requisition succeeded in ensuring our superiority.

It should be added that this great requisition encountered fewer difficulties than the recruitment of three hundred thousand men in the preceding March. The revolutionary movement had spread, and the republican idea that every citizen owes service to his country had won people's minds.

However, it was not with tumultuous bands that France would have conquered Europe; the nation had to be transformed into an army.

It was then that the activity of Carnot was deployed above all.

It was a question of organising, according to the principle of unity, a multitude as not homogeneous in its elements as in its constitution.

It was made up of former soldiers and conscripts brought in, either by the levy of three hundred thousand men, or by the levy *en masse*, not to mention the volunteers of all dates, the remains of the free companies and foreigners.

Certain corps had remained as before the Revolution, while several generals had formed theirs in demi-brigade according to the new mode; then there were French or foreign legions, a mixture of all kinds of weapons. There were seasoned, experienced battalions, others entirely novices; there were considerable differences in size between corps of the same species; there were irregularly acquired and exaggerated numbers; soldiers recruited in haste, without their being fit for service; the states were almost completely lacking. As for the irregularity of the supplies and the accounts, it would be hard to imagine what it was.

How was this chaos cleared? this is what we could not say without overloading a simple biography with details which belong to the general history of the French Army.

What is certain is that this army soon became the most homogeneous in Europe.

To erase all external distinction was one of the first objects of concern. The line troops had largely kept the old white uniform, while the new arrivals wore the national dress: a fertile source of misunderstanding. From August 29th, a decree prescribed the unity of the costume.

The engineering weapon received a new organisation, which Carnot took special care of. The numerous companies of volunteer gunners, who had been formed and remarkably well trained, were incorporated into the artillery. We even managed to improvise a cavalry. The shortage of horses was extreme: purchases made in all the foreign countries where our agents were able to penetrate, an extraordinary levy in the cantons and the *arrondissements* of the Republic, and numerous spontaneous donations, made it possible to put in line riders capable of to measure with the formidable squadrons of the allies.

In February 1792, France had only 228,000 men (204,000 under arms); before May, thanks to the activity deployed, it numbered 471,000 soldiers (present 397,000); to July 15th, 479,000, if we refer to a note from Saint-Just, kept for his own instruction, and of which we have the autograph. The official table that we consult presents a figure which deviates little from it, 483,000 (registered, 599,000).

In December, the strength of the army stood at 628,000 men (present under the flag, 554,000). This number grew to 1,026,000 (732,000 on combat ground in September 1794). There is no serious reason to dispute these statements, published at a time when exaggeration could benefit nothing (1797).

However, it has been said that the republican phalanges never numbered more than 600,000 men, one writer reduced them to 500,000, another to 400,000, adding that they were neither armed, nor fed, nor clothed. Do we hope, by such assertions, to belittle the merits of revolutionary dictators? on the contrary, it is raised. The fewer resources they are supposed to have in their hands, the more admirable the result obtained will appear:

Nothing can erase this historical truth, that the Convention found the enemy thirty leagues from Paris, and that due to its prodigious efforts to conclude peace thirty leagues from Vienna.

It is Benjamin Constant who says this: Benjamin Constant is a spirit of 1791; a supporter of principles, he was generally little admirer of the facts of the Revolution.

2: EXTRACT FROM THE MEMOIRS OF CARNOT
LIFT OF THE MAUBEUGE BLOCKADE AND BATTLE OF WATIGNIES

Alarming news was coming from the north.

Despite the victory of Hondschoote, who promised to give the French Armies a decisive preponderance, but which General Houchard had not been able to take advantage of, the situation made by Norwinde had changed little. Le Quesnoy was in the hands of the allies; already masters of Valenciennes and Condé, they owned the Scheldt; their ambition was now to also dominate the Sambre, by seizing Maubeuge, which would have become their base of operations. This fallen square, nothing seriously stopped their march towards the capital.

On September 29th, the Prince of Cobourg forced the passage of the river by six columns, invested Maubeuge, and carried his Army of Observation on Avesnes and Landrecies.

The rather mediocre place de Maubeuge was covered by an entrenched camp, advantageously situated, where twenty thousand men had just rallied, who found themselves blocked at the same time. Perhaps the Austrian general had committed an imprudence in allowing this imposing force to be grouped together, the unfortunate immobility of which he could not foresee. But he was aware that the city's supplies would soon be insufficient for such numerous mouths. The troops, in fact, were at first reduced to half a ration: at the end of a few days the famine was complete. Diseases broke out, and the hospitals no longer being able to contain the sick, they had to be deposited under the hangars of the suburbs. However, the besiegers raised formidable works, three batteries of twenty pieces of 24, and the circle of their cannons was so tightened that the cannonballs passed whistling above the entrenched camp, to bring death and destruction to the city. Many inhabitants of the surroundings had taken refuge there, and they increased the alarms, telling of the looting of their farms and the burning of their homes.

Three commissioners of the Convention endeavoured to support the courage. They wanted to inform the government of Maubeuge's critical situation: one of them, Drouet, from the first moments of the blockade, tried, with more daring than prudence, to cross the enemy lines: he was taken and went to expiate in the dungeons remember Varennes. A few days later, thirteen dragoons devoted themselves; they swam across the Sambre and managed to reach Philippeville.

But the Republic had not waited for this distress call to help its children, the saviours were approaching. On the evening of October 14th to 15th, the besieged heard, through the fire of the Austrians, a cannonade further away. They did not yet dare to indulge themselves in the joy, some fearing that this noise would announce the bombardment of Avesnes, others fearing a trap of the enemy to attract our soldiers out of the camp and bring them to grips with an army that would crush them with its superiority. In the midst of these uncertainties, the defenders of Maubeuge remained inactive, and did not second, as they might have done, the efforts of their liberators.

Because this cannonade was indeed that of the French Army, which came to the aid of the city. Here's what happened:

The important and rapid military operations which were to be carried out in the North had made felt the need for a younger and stronger hand than that of Houchard. Carnot, witness to Jourdan's fine conduct at Hondschoote, appointed him to the Committee. His choice having been ratified, he himself went to the new general to bring him his commission, which united under his command the available forces of the Armies of the North and the Ardennes. Jourdan sketched out a project, which Carnot approved in his main data, and which was used later, but which did not appear to him to be related to the imminence of the danger. Back in the Committee, he proposed to go directly attack the enemy in his formidable position, in order to deliver Maubeuge; this was almost a matter of life and death for the Republic. His colleagues found the enterprise too daring to entrust it to a general who was in command for the first time, and they only consented to adopt it on condition that Carnot himself would take it over.

He didn't even give himself time to go and say goodbye to his family. He left in the night, after having sent a courier to Péronne, where his brother Feulins resided, foreseeing that he would need him for some sort of dedication. At Carnot's request, he was assigned the conventional Duquesnoy, who had so well assisted him in the attack on Furnes, and who was also going to find his brother under the walls of Maubeuge. All, as well as Jourdan, met in Péronne on October 7th, and they moved to Guise, place of the general meeting, which took from there the name of Réunion-sur-Oise. Carnot writes:

> The soldiers have confidence in him and ask only to fight; we hope not to make them languish. The matter will be hot; but we will win and the homeland will be saved.
> We would need at least fifteen thousand bayonets to charge the enemy French style.

After a conference between Jourdan and the commissioners of the Assembly, the *quartier général* was quickly brought from Guise to Avesnes, two leagues from the outposts of the Prince of Cobourg.

Forty-five thousand soldiers approximately, drawn from the camps of Gavarelle, Cassel and Lille, made up the French Army where the new levies were still very imperfectly organised: Cobourg had from seventy-five to eighty thousand men, divided in two corps, one of investment (forty thousand at least), around Maubeuge; the other for observation (thirty-five thousand), to the south of this town, in the positions of Wattignies, Doulers, Saint-Rémy and other villages, along a small tributary of the Sambre, the Tarsy. Strongly posted on heights bristling with batteries, covered by palisaded ditches by very high hedges, by immense cuts of trees overturned with their branches, and all the roads being broken, the Austrians seemed in such an impregnable position.

This bravado was carried to the other camp, where it strongly stimulated national self-esteem. Our soldiers repeated to themselves cheerfully that they would go and summon Citizen Cobourg to keep his word.

The next day, October 14th, reconnaissance of the enemy positions by Jourdan and Carnot, shooting started on the line and ended with a few cannon shots, which resounded as far as Maubeuge and brought hope to the hearts of the besieged.

On the morning of the 15th, the French set off: Fromentin's division, detached from the left wing, advanced by the old Roman road from Reims to Bavai, towards the village of Monceau. In the centre, General Balland, with several batteries of 16 and 12, emerges through the Avesnes hedge, a very uneven ground covered with wood (it is now pasture) and comes to occupy the heights in front of Doulers and

Saint-Aubin. General Duquesnoy, brother of the deputy, commanded the right, took possession of the village of Beugnies. The headquarters are brought to the point where the road from Soire-le-Château branches off with that from Avesnes to Maubeuge.

The planned operations had for support the places of Rocroy, Marienbourg, Philippeville, and the detachments which advanced on this side by the orders of Jourdan: for we have said that, in these grave circumstances, the Committee had placed the Army of Ardennes at its disposal.

Towards seven o'clock in the morning, the general-in-chief advances, accompanied by the two representatives of the Convention. The signal to attack is given on all points at the same time. The plan adopted had as its goal, wherever victorious, to rush towards Maubeuge to join hands with the entrenched camp. But in the event of a setback, we always kept the road to Guise. The two wings were to march quickly, while in the centre, at Doulers, we would limit ourselves to a cannonade. Batteries posted in front of this village dismantled those which the enemy had established beyond, behind the dwellings bordering the main road. The cannon balls of the two artillery crossed over the village located mid-coast. Several of our pieces, served by the brave gunners of the commune of Paris, worked wonders.

Everything seemed to go at first as desired: General Fromentin, at the head of twelve thousand infantry, dislodged the Austrian skirmishers from the heights which crown the villages of Saint-Remy and Saint-Waast. Duquesnoy was also gaining ground on the right; master of Dimont and Dimechaux, he was already beginning to fire against Wattignies. Our wings seemed to have joined by a concentric movement, which put the enemy army in the greatest peril.

At the news of these successes, capable of bringing the total loss of the Austrians, the cannonade of Doulers was transformed into a full force attack. The business was difficult. Balland's division (about thirteen thousand men) saw on all the highest points beyond the village, already powerfully defended, a mass of threatening guns, and on all the roads an eager cavalry to rush forward.

Nothing, however, made the republicans hesitate: they ran to the enemy singing the *Marseillaise*, having at their head, with the general-in-chief, the representatives of the people, whose example excited them; they rushed over the first obstacles on the ground, penetrated the village with bayonets and seized the castle; they were about to climb the heights which are beyond the valley of the Bracquière, when a terrible grape-shot stopped them. Threatened at the same time by the cavalry ready to charge on their flanks, they were forced to abandon the positions conquered with so much heroism.

The rapidity with which these positions had been taken by our young soldiers, however, allowed great hopes for a second attempt. Their momentum was irresistible. The commissioners of the Assembly wanted to take advantage of it. The general swayed. Carnot, in a movement of impatience, let escape these words: "Not too much prudence, general!"—Jourdan, wounded to the quick (and precisely wounded, it must be admitted), immediately gives the signal for a new attack, and made it supported by a column of cavalry, charged with turning the position. This cavalry finds all the exits barricaded. During this time the assault begins again: same efforts, same success at first, same fatal outcome.

This time, it was Jourdan, piqued for honour, who absolutely wanted to return to the charge, but without better result: the Austrians had just received reinforcements from their right, where our affairs had turned sour.

General Fromentin, intoxicated by his first advantages, instead of walking along the edge of the large Leroy wood, as he had been recommended to do, in order to be able to take shelter against the superior cavalry of the enemy, had imprudently ventured in the plain of Berlaimont, with troops of the new levy; the Austrian squadrons, suddenly emerging from the woods of Doulers, assailed them and threw panic and rout into their ranks.

As soon as this unfortunate news was known in the centre, we had to give up the attack of Doulers, calculated on the progress of the two wings. The plan had to be changed, which Fromentin's failure had compromised.

Jourdan's first cry was this: "Let's go to the help of the left wing!" the order had already been given, when Carnot arrived: "General," he said eagerly, "here is how one loses a battle!" and the order was revoked.

Night had come, the shooting ceased; the two armies bivouacked on the battlefield.

The council having assembled, Jourdan developed his opinion: according to the principles of the old war, he proposed to abandon all thought of attack on the centre of the enemy, and to direct forces towards our left wing, in order to restore balance, there. Carnot maintained, on the contrary, that it was necessary to recall the Fromentin division, and to concentrate our efforts on the right, already in the process of success, a manoeuvre which preserved for us the advantages of the offensive, so important for young soldiers, little suited to the chances of success. the war. "What does it matter," he cried, "whether we enter Maubeuge from the right or from the left?"

"Is that where we must triumph?" he added, putting his finger on the map at Wattignies point. Wattignies being closer than Doulers to the town and the camp, this position removed, the other became unimportant. Moreover, the detached bodies of the Ardennes Army, which were advancing under the orders of Generals Elie and Beauregard, towards the extreme left of the enemy, would soon find themselves in a position to support the movement proposed by Carnot.

"If we yield to the opinion of the representative of the people," said Jourdan, "I warn him that he takes responsibility for it."

"I take care of everything, and even of the execution," cried Carnot with an ardour which drew the council. Jourdan had the good spirit to make the idea he had just fought his own, and supported it with as much.

Carnot counted on the nature of a very steep and very wooded ground, which would hide our march, and which, this uncovered march, would make it possible to defend itself with not very considerable forces, supported by the place of Avesnes. He also counted on the known character of the German general, who would never presume, on the part of his adversaries, a manoeuvre so far removed from the strategy in use, and from which one could hardly expect a bold and improvised move either.

It should be added that a happy coincidence favoured the French: a thick fog, a frequent phenomenon in this season, arose between them and the one who had so much interest in observing their movement; it lasted until about noon. Behind this curtain, six or seven thousand men, starting from the centre and the left, passed to the right; this manoeuvre gave our army a direction perpendicular to that which it had had the day before. The Prince of Cobourg, who believed us in the old arrangement, had changed nothing in his. During the same time; General Beauregard, after having seized the villages of Berelles and Eccles, came to position himself behind Obrechies, to second the attack which was being planned.

In order to better confuse the enemy, Generals Balland and Fromentin kept up the fire of their batteries near Doulers, pretending to want to renew the attempts of the day before, while Jourdan and the representatives of the people marched to the plateau of Wattignies, which was going become the goal of a concentric effort. Twenty-four thousand men were going to fight there. The Austrians were stunned when the fog having broken, a splendid sun showed them a mass of attackers climbing towards them with the cry of '*Vive la République!*' Carnot and Duquesnoy were advancing at the head of one of the three attacking columns, their representative hats on the tips of their sabres.

The position of the Austrians was very strong. The village of Wattignies, which gave its name to the battle, is located on a high plateau surrounded by deep valleys and rivers, and these natural obstacles had been further increased by numerous entrenchments. The plateau itself is dominated by the heights of Clarye, now cultivated, but then covered with heather and also occupied by the enemy.

The French infantry marched, supported by field batteries, the cannon balls of which opened the way for them. A historian (Toulongeon), said:

> According to the Austrians, they had never seen such a terrible execution of artillery. They said they heard, during the detonations of the guns, resounding in the republican ranks the bellicose songs and the patriotic airs.

However, the enemy's fire was neither less well nourished, nor less murderous than ours; General Duquesnoy's skirmishers, driven back, knocked down, strafed with grape-shot, retreated. At this moment Colonel Carnot-Feulins saw a battalion of new recruits which had taken refuge in a fold of the ground, sheltered from the blows, the soldiers grouped around their commander, "like chickens frightened by a bird of prey." This is the expression my uncle used when relating this episode. After having ordered them in vain to march, Carnot-Feulins seizes the officer by the collar of his coat and leads him at the step of his horse into the grape-shot; the battalion, which followed it, redeems by a vigorous charge this minute of cowardice.

Twice the French are pushed back with considerable losses. Finally, a general assault seems to give us victory everywhere at the same time: Fromentin forces his adversary Bellegarde to abandon the redoubts of Saint-Waast and Saint-Aubin; Balland drives out the Bohemian grenadiers from the heights of Doulers, which struck down Wattignies; our skirmishers redouble their efforts. The village of Wattignies is taken and retaken with the bayonet, despite the hedges and palisades which surround these gardens; three Austrian regiments are annihilated; the enemy withdrew in disorder to the heights of Clarye, where he found a still dangerous position for the victors.

Cobourg understood the new plan of his adversaries; he has recalled a portion of his right wing towards the centre, and at the moment when a French brigade, under the orders of General Gratien, advances by firing in the middle of the heather, the imperial cavalrymen run on it with their sword high; it does not support the shock, it dislodges and opens a large gap, through which the horses rush. The general himself commands the retreat.

This act of weakness and disobedience (for Gratien had formal orders which prescribed him to go forward), could demoralize our soldiers and compromise all their advantages. Carnot, the eldest, notices this, he rushes towards the Gratien brigade, has it put in line on a high plateau, in sight of the whole army, and solemnly dismisses the chief who had just retreated in front of the enemy, then he jumps off his horse and forms this brigade into an assault column.

At this moment his gaze discovers a poor conscript, huddled behind a hedge and trembling with all his limbs, Carnot approaches him, picks up his rifle, discharges it on the enemy, then brings the young man back and places him in the ranks. Then taking the weapon of a wounded grenadier, he walks at the head of a column, while his colleague Duquesnoy, like him dressed in the national scarf and the representative's costume, advances with Jourdan at the head of the other. The soldiers, ashamed of their flight, want to erase their memory by redoubling their courage in the presence of the commissioners of the Assembly: they rush forward with impetuosity.

Colonel Carnot-Feulins is currently making a decisive manoeuvre: he quickly carries a battery of twelve pieces on the flank of the Austrian cavalry, which had just done us so much harm: his fire, well directed, overthrows the squadrons. The enemy stops, retreats and flees in the direction of Beaufort. The position, this time, was removed.

The two representatives of the people at the same time reached the top of the plateau; both victorious, they embraced in the eyes of the intoxicated soldiers, and an immense cry of '*Vive la République!*' taught the French Army its triumph, the enemy its defeat.

Beautiful day, which drew this patriotic exclamation from an emigrant, Chateaubriand:

The French recovered at Wattignies that brilliant courage which

131

they seemed to have lost since Jemmapes.

We saw them rushing forward with that ardour which distinguishes their first charge from that of other peoples.

The same evening, the Prince of Cobourg, judging it prudent not to wait for a second shock from these Republican soldiers, whom he described as enraged in his bulletin, decided to return to the Sambre, although his lieutenants, Haddick and Benjowski, would have obtained rather notable advantages on the left wing, over the French generals Élie and Beauregard, and although the Duke of York hastened to his aid, which perhaps would have turned the odds in his favour. A fog like that which had favoured our happy evolution the day before covered that which the enemy had to make to put himself out of our reach. He had lost three thousand men, and we were half that number.

Many officers had distinguished themselves: among them the brave d'Hautpoul, killed later at Eylau, and Mortier, future marshal of France, wounded in the attack on Doulers. The latter received from Carnot, while he was being dressed in the ambulance, the rank of adjutant-general. As for the soldiers, Jourdan's report sums up their conduct in one word:

"They were so many heroes!"

Night had covered the battlefield. Carnot, estranged from his family, deprived of his mount, exhausted with needs and weariness, had remained alone, tormented by the thought that his presence might be necessary at headquarters to stop the arrangements for the next day; for he was still ignorant of the enemy's flight. Fortunately, he was met by a detachment of cavalry, whose leader made him accept his horse and escort him to Avesnes. The alarm had already spread there: it was feared that one of the representatives of the Assembly was among the dead, and they had sent to his discovery

A local historian says:

On the 17th, the victors of Wattignies were following the course of the Sambre and entering Maubeuge, in the midst of transports of frenzied joy. The smoke of the gunpowder, the dust of the bivouacs, as well as the disorder of their clothes— added to the assurance which victory procures, gave them a martial and terrible air, which contrasted with the despondency and the spite of the troops of the camp, ashamed of their inaction, and not knowing how to respond to the bitter reproaches addressed to them!

Without this deplorable inaction, in fact, our victory would have been much more complete, and all the enemy's artillery would probably have fallen into our hands.

The Convention and the entire Republic joined their grateful acclamations to those of the inhabitants of Maubeuge: the Revolution had just escaped one of its greatest perils.

Carnot left for Paris immediately; and, two days later, he wrote to the army to congratulate it on its triumph, without giving it to be understood, even indirectly, that he had been a spectator and an actor. He did not seem to have left his office.

3: Extract from a Military Memoir on Kehl, by a senior Army officer. Strasbourg, Levrault, 1797

Kehl Evacuation

Thus ends, after fifty days of open trenches and a hundred and fifteen days of investment, one of the memorable sieges that history can offer. Indeed, we see on the one hand an Army of seventy seasoned battalions, proud of having forced their enemy to retreat, deploying the entire apparatus of a large siege against shapeless entrenchments, supplementing the daring that misses him by the immensity of his works, making the siege of some detached works, deploying a formidable artillery against the hovels occupied by skirmishers; nevertheless his adversary disputes the ground foot to foot; it is forced to assault every part of the work where it wishes to lodge and loses in detail more soldiers than a general attack would have cost it.

On the other side, a place built in haste, in earth, of which only a few parts are covered, without buildings, without stores, without shelters; linked to an entrenched camp of a large development, but whose main defences consisting of puddles and marshes are reduced to nothing by frost. In truth, it has the advantage of not being able to be entirely blocked and of maintaining easy communication with Strasbourg, which imposes enough on the enemy to urge him to leave nothing to chance: although defended by exhausted troops of a long retreat, to which one cannot provide the most indispensable articles of clothing and relief, the term of his defence far exceeds that which could have been prescribed . . . . Almost all the palisades were overturned, the ditches filled in part by the landslides of the parapets, and the arrival of reinforcements became very difficult . . . We therefore decided to evacuate . . . We hardly had more than twenty-four hours to remove everything. Nevertheless, such activity was put into it that not a single palisade was left to the enemy; everything was brought back to the right bank, to the fragments of bombs and shells, and to the woods of the platforms.

French Uniforms

(Armies of Sambre-et-Meuse and Rhine-et-Moselle)

I particularly wanted to give with this journal drawings of French uniforms whose authenticity was equal to that of the text. Although not yet a century had passed since 1792, it was difficult. It is easier to find the exact dress of a fifteenth century infantryman than that of a soldier of the Army of the Rhine-and-Moselle. After looking for it in vain in France, it was in Germany that I found them, thanks to my colleague Raffet, from the Cabinet of Prints of the National Library.

To know certain secrets of Parisian life, it is often necessary to read the correspondence of foreign newspapers. Similarly, you have to see the German engravings from 1792 to 1802 to get an idea of the behaviour of our troops in the countryside. Nothing more unforeseen nor more disjointed; one can easily imagine the surprise of the good Germans accustomed to correcting the behaviour and movements of armies disciplined in the Prussian style. Their designers immediately wanted to fix the memory; they did not hide anything torn clothes, tattered shirts, shoes with holes; they laid bare all the miseries of these starving conquerors, whom they often personify in the person of a thin infantryman opening his mouth to swallow this round ball which represents the world, with the inscription: *he will go there* .

The Germans must have cruelly felt the presence of these bands which generally lived on their conquests, and yet they could not give their oppressors a ferocious air. As much as they lend a grumpy expression to their armed compatriots, they keep an air of smiling at these frenzied people who absolutely want to drink their wine and dance with their daughters, not without lavishing them with the most cavalier caresses. They probably even wanted to shame the weaknesses of women who ended up smiling at these beggars, because one of their favourite caricatures represents French uniform pants, each leg of which is pulled in the opposite direction by two rival gossips. Other favourite subjects are the departure of the regiment, the women in tears,

It must be admitted that the seducers had nothing but appearance for them and that they needed a prodigious kindness to hide the disasters of their uniform. Talented artists have, after the fact, naturalised in France a *correct* type of the republican soldier; he wears moustaches, has an uncovered neck, a black tie; his hat is on *in a column* and his pants have pink stripes; but in reality, it is less charming. First of all, the horned hat, considered awkward, is combed crassly like that of the *gendarmes*, and most often backwards, well behind, cockade and plume on the side of the back. The loop of the cockade serves as a rack for various small objects. Sometimes the pipe is passed through; sometimes the spoon and the fork with two tips cross there like a gourmet pompom.

Sometimes the spoon changes position and elegantly passes through two buttonholes on the back of the coat. The helmet and the hussar cap are also thrown back from the head. The moustache is an exception. The tie goes up very high, twists several times and its ends fall with a big knot on the *buffleteries*. This strong tie, almost always striped, is more often yellowish than black. As we will see, the coat buttoned little and the elbows, sometimes with holes, gave a sad idea of the whiteness that the lapels and the waistcoat might have retained.

The trousers are bridged, more or less well buttoned; if it is striped, its stripes affect all layouts and colours; the checks, the diamonds, the welts are noticeable in the uniforms of the volunteers, and some officers, who carry the backpack on their backs like their soldiers, have real sticky hose, horizontally striped in red, white and blue, held in place by underwear. Very long feet which reach for the pants above the ankle. The shoes, a page of which we have purposely filled, are almost always in the saddest condition; a *chasseur à pied*, which we reproduce later, seems to have no more than soles fixed by thongs. Another has completely bare feet.

The cavalry is not yet in the clothes with short sides, even in certain regiments of hussars, it remains faithful to the long panels decorated with piping and strong buttons; the sheepskin which protects some pants has Greek contours; the bonnet of the hussars is topped with a plume almost as long, and the visor-less helmet of the dragons disappears with part of the face under a dishevelled mane that gives them a fierce appearance. The artillery is distinguished only by its full dress of blue cloth; his severe appearance is enhanced by the red *soutaches* of the waistcoat in the mounted artillery.

The haversack of many soldiers does not have the regular shape of today. It is an ordinary bag in leather or brown canvas, tightened at the throat by a string, held in place by straps; and it almost descends on the patient's kidneys, which must have increased the weight.

A single soldier wears the long flame police cap with a truly military haversack, but the straps of which hold a whole world. At the top is a goose; his neck is tightened by the strap, and his head falls melancholy in the direction of a pot dangling at the height of the cartridge. The centre is crossed out by a long loaf, and a bottle hangs on the right side. We see that the assortment is complete and that our Zouaves have not invented anything. The officers have pistols on their belts, and wear the *gorget* held in place by a chain or by a longer cord than has been worn since; it is with the sabre the only insignia which announces the rank on the long campaign hood. Almost all of the drummers are children or adolescents; as an age, Barras was no exception.

I have spoken of the surprise caused on the other side of the Rhine by the appearance of the Republican Armies. We can hardly believe that it was translated in a flattering way for our weapons, and that in the very heart of the German countries. Nothing is more certain, however, when one can be confronted with a sort of album, oblong quarto printed in Leipzig in 1794 on behalf of the bookseller Friedrich August Leo. The German and French text is preceded by the following two general titles:

Abbildung und Beschreibung Verschiedener Truppen des französischen army, mit illuminirten Kupfern .

Representation and description of different troops of the French Army, with coloured plates.

The text is in two columns. Here is the specific title of the French part:

Description of the few bodies making up the (French) Armies, by an eyewitness. *Leipzig, bei Friedrich August Leo*, 1794.

This description seemed to us so interesting and even so surprising from a political point of view that we reproduce it in full here. Its relation to our subject is direct, and the details given are of a precious accuracy.

The German author expresses himself in these terms:

"The energy, the bravery and the constancy with which the French troops are waging a war which has not yet seen an example in history, should make any head think about which the interests of this lower world are not indifferent.

"How many things up to now have we taken on word essential for an army to make it victorious and which the French Armies have been doing for four years?

"The severe discipline that Frederick II had introduced among his troops has made many imitators and found an infinity of supporters. Deceived by appearance, we imagined that the severity pushed to the most inhuman constraint, made automata invincible or victorious. We would have judged it very differently in the days of Frédéric's success, if we had had the word of the enigma.

"The present war is well capable of destroying a prevention which generally makes each soldier a devoted victim to the blows of sticks from a whole scale of superiors.

"Everywhere it is claimed that armies act and everywhere the soldier is a passive creature who can neither move nor act. In garrison, the soldier is accustomed to humiliating himself under the baton, and when there is war, they claim that he is sensitive to the affront of a defeat, the shame of which never falls on him.

"It is, however, with men thus degraded that we claim to conquer troops which know no differences between individuals except those of the functions entrusted to them; of discipline than the duty of the degree in which each is placed, and of subordination that imposed by law and the advantage of the service. By debasing man, we will never make him do great things; It is only by showing him that he is worthy of this honour that one makes him want to acquire it.

"Men are what we make them. It is up to those who employ them to know how to handle them, to train them as they should be to fulfil what is expected of them. But we should not expect that they will be interested in making successful projects that do not offer them any advantageous prospect for themselves or theirs against men who have given themselves a way of being that they find good and that they believe they have the right to defend against and against all.

"Between princes, war is a game of chance where the last crown decides. Between princes and nation, it is the lion wrapped in a net: the mouse is not always there to gnaw the mesh. We sometimes lose sight of the fact that we can do nothing if we are not supported by this general agreement which makes all wills fly towards the same goal. To want to act in this state of error is to expose oneself to disgrace, or at most to ephemeral successes. This is what the experience of all time proves. The princes create armies, but how much trouble and expense it costs them . . . how many private interests must be spared in raising recruits! How long is it before these new levies can go into the field! The evil is not great if it is against a prince that the we are at war. On the contrary, is it against a nation? She gets up and walks, and it's easy to see which side will be the advantage.

"A nation raised in this way, it is true, does not have that flattering look that an old regiment offers when it is ranged in parade, where all the soldiers seem to be cast in the same mould. This rigorous uniformity imposes it, but it is not, as we see now, indispensable to victory. The National Guard is no less courageous, although irregularly dressed, than those of this line, where this regularity is observed more exactly.

"Animated by the same spirit, these various troops fight with the same bravery, brave death with the same courage, endure in common work and fatigue.

"We therefore dare to believe that the public will not see with indifference the image of some of the bodies of which the republican armies are composed. The illuminated figures are portrayed as natural as seen by an eyewitness. We contented ourselves with multiplying copies without changing anything.

"The dragoons do a very different service in France than in the armies of other sovereigns. They are placed on the wings, in outposts, at the crossings of rivers, in defiles or at bridgeheads. But their real place, on a battle day, is in the reserve corps, because of the speed with which they can be moved and the vivacity with which they charge the enemy. They are still employed in various ways in sieges and in an infinite number of cases in which they are made to supply the infantry as well as the cavalry. Also, they are also made to learn the exercises of these two weapons. Until the end of the Seven Years' War, they were dressed in red; but since then, we have dressed them in green. Their uniform is: green coat, red cuffs, lapels, collar and lining, white jacket and breeches or doe belly, polished brass helmet surmounted by a tuft of black horsehair hanging from the back of the head, soft boots and curved sabres. Their horses are usually four feet to four feet two inches. On horseback, their weapons are a rifle, two pistols, and the sabre; on foot, they have only the rifle and the sabre. Only young people who are vigorous, nimble, well made, and who show great skill are admitted.

"The *chasseur* grenadiers (horse grenadiers) owed their first creation to Louis XIV. In order to enable the reader to judge of which men this troop has always been composed, it is because, in order to train it, each grenadier captain was required to provide a man of the required size, generally recognised as strong and brave and with a moustache. This *esprit de corps*, this unfailing courage have never wavered. Their uniform is dark blue, scarlet cuffs, lapels and collar, white buttons on which is printed the tree of liberty with the cap and around the inscription: *République Française*; white jacket and white breeches of silver and also breeches of skin. Fur cap with red background, braided cords and strainers in national colours. In the middle of the forehead, a plaque on which is embossed the constitutional seal with trophies and on each side of the plaque a flaming grenade. The hair of these hats is turned up and down, so that the rainwater does not stop there. The lining of the coat is white serge.

"At the bottom of the sides where the hooks are to roll them up, there is a pomegranate of red cloth, and, instead of a flame, there are small tassels which descend from it hanging from cords of the same colour. They have aiguillettes braided in red and white, black collars, soft boots, but strong knee pads. Their weapons are the rifle, two pistols, and a sabre whose straight blade is nearly two inches wide and terminates in a very sharp point, the double edge of which is about eight inches long, and the whole sabre between forty and forty-five. They wear it over the shoulder. They have a brown leather cartridge holder with a white plaque embossed with the tree of liberty with the cap, but without the inscription. Finally, they have a large blue coat lined with a red cord, with a wide flap that serves as a hood. In action, especially when they are attacked, they lower themselves very front on their horses and know how to use the point of their sabre, to the handling of which they apply themselves singularly in their moments of leisure, which gives them a decisive advantage over their enemies, who do not have the same dexterity or the same speed even though they would have the same bravery.

"The *Chasseurs à Cheval* are of modern creation and form a very large cavalry in the French Armies. Their service approaches that of the dragoons, except that they are more commonly employed in discovery; to beat the woods always in front of the army. Their uniform is a dark green coat with a straight collar, white cuffs, lapels and buttons like those of the horse grenadiers, leather breeches and a white jacket. Their slightly short coat has white lining, long pockets with three buttons on the legs. They wear soft boots, knee pads alike. It is not possible to give an exact description of their cap or helmet. It has the shape of the freedom cap, it is of heavily beaten leather and topped with a tuft of horsehair or bear skin the width of the hand. This hairstyle is surrounded by a strip of yellow and tiger oilcloth. On each side, a brass chain which, going up, forms an acute angle. Around the neck they have collars or black ties. The lower officers are distinguished in this body as in that of the mounted grenadiers by a few loops on the sleeves, but which in this body are braided with the national colours. Their weapons are the carbine snap hook, two pistols, a long brass-mounted sabre with an eight-inch double-edged point. They wear it slung over a leather belt. The cartridge holder is of black leather with a yellow plaque and the constitutional seal in relief. They have coats in the colour of the habit: both are edged with a red cord. They have horses with twelve to thirteen palms. It is the largest part of the cavalry.

"Nothing has been changed to the rest of the cavalry, the fit and weapons are the same, except for the buttons which are like those of grenadiers and *chasseurs*; the riders have a cockade with a tricolour *aigrette* on their hat.

"The clothing of the *chasseurs* on foot is little different from that of the *chasseurs à cheval,* except that the coat is longer and goes to the knees. They have the same helmets, as well as jackets and breeches; and very light cowhide boots. The lower officers have two *epaulettes* to distinguish them from ordinary *chasseurs*. Their weapons are a rifle with a bayonet and a sabre like that of the grenadiers they carry over their shoulder. The cartridge holder is of black leather with a yellow plate with the arms of the fatherland. The hunters and the line troops form the *élite* of the infantry. There are a number of professional *chasseurs* per battalion or company, armed with rifles and daggers; instead of pouches, they have a flask (powder pair). They are distinguished from the others by a red collar on the coat and a tricolour *epaulette* on the right shoulder. This troop renders very great services in that it is also specific to the service of the troops of the line and the light troops.

"It is not easy to give an exact description of the National Guards nor to put them in any class. But one must be convinced that they fight well, although there are some who are dressed only in jackets and shirts, canvas smocks or clothes of any colour, quilted jackets or jackets. Indian, and pants anyway. Most, however, have dark blue clothes with red or white collars, yellow or white buttons, with the cap or the tree of liberty imprinted. In part, they wear *gamaches* or gaiters; many wear shoes and silk stockings; but all generally wear small objects on their hats which allude to Liberty and Equality. They all have a rifle and a bayonet; some have cartridge-holders, others have none, it is the same with the sword. Instead of a haversack, they have a pocket bag in which to carry their clothes.

"We now call *legion* troops of French farmers, part requisitioned and part people of good will. Their clothing is none other than the ordinary clothing of country people. They are wearing bonnets, hats of different shapes, but always with the national cockade. All of them have blue stockings with a garter buckled so that the stockings make a sort of small bead near the knee. Their pants are all different from each other: from cloth, canvas of all kinds of colour to black skin. Their shoes are closed with blue or black ties. Their weapons are the spear or the pike, the handle of which is about six feet long and painted in the national colours. Some have a rifle with the bayonet. Others have a belt around their body, to the left of which a pistol is attached. These are mostly those who wear spikes. Many have parade swords, daggers or other bladed weapons hanging from their side.

"There are one or two legions with each army, depending on how large the army is. Each legion is about seven thousand strong. These are officers and low officers drawn from the invalids who command them, along with a few others whom they themselves elected from among themselves. Each legion has a brigadier general or brigadier.

"These legions receive neither bread nor pay; they provide for their maintenance themselves. The men are held there for one year of service; they never show themselves in the open country and do not line up in battle. They do not stop worrying the enemy armies a lot."

Plates

1

Général de Division

Tricolour plume surmounting three red feathers. Blue coat with red turned-down collar; gold braid on the hat, sleeves, pockets and collar. White pants, black boots; red scarf with golden fringe. Golden strap on the sabre hilt; the scabbard is lined with gilded copper.

This young figure should come as no surprise at the time when a simple officer could pass four ranks in twenty-four hours and immediately lose command if he did not justify this confidence by a victory.

2

Adjudant Général

"In campaign clothes," says the legend. The golden belt, the hat with feathers and tassels contrast a little with the severity of this long blue hood with a turned-down red collar. But it was good that the adjutant general was seen by everyone, because he was a real chief of staff, ranked hierarchically below the brigadier general, but above the colonel.

3

Hussard

Black shako surrounded by a flame of black cloth with blue piping. Green and red plume. White cord with tassel falling to the right
of the shako. Brown-brown Dolman with white *soutache* and black
filling. Blue pants with white braid. Orange sabretache with copper
ornaments. Black half boots.

The pronounced inclination of the shako seems a little forced by
the dimensions of the plume: they are such that the balance would be
compromised if the vertical was kept.

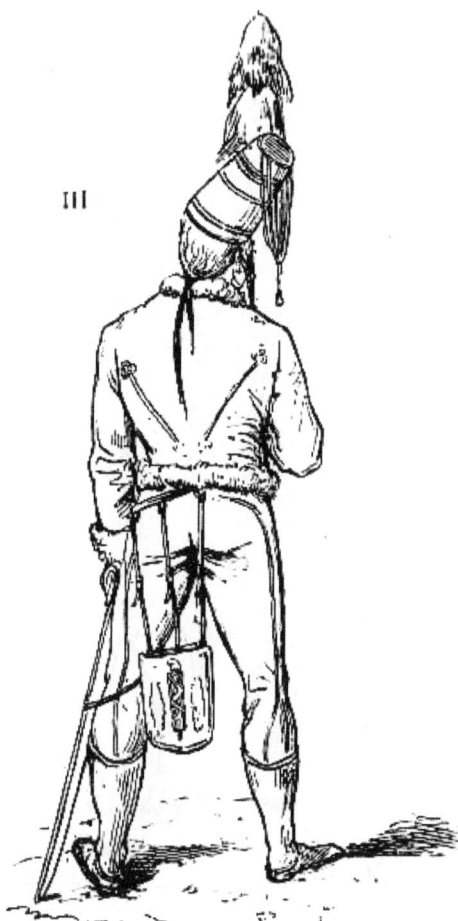

III

4

Infantry Officers and Soldiers

The officer wears a red plume. Blue coat with red collar and cuffs. White lapels with red hairline. White waistcoat and tights. Backpack. Golden collar rise. The right hand is supported by a cane.

The infantryman behind him wears black gaiters and nankeen breeches. Blue coat with white lapels.

The furry bonnet of the grenadier is too reminiscent of that of the Austrian grenadiers not to have been taken from an enemy store. What would confirm in this idea is that it is obviously too narrow for the head of our man. White and red striped vest; white and blue striped tie; it frames the chin like a *cravat à la Garat*. Red epaulet; tricolour plume; nankeen pants. Same dress as the previous one.

5

Infantry Soldier

This offers a specimen of the neglected genre. He wears the same coat and the same hat, but his bluish checkered trousers have a different heavy piece of material at the knee. Of the shoes, he kept only the soles on which the cut upper acts as sandal straps. No vest. Loose tie. The open suit allows the shirt to slip through.

6

Cavaliers

Blue coat with red lapels. White collar, breeches and *buffleteries*. Black boots and hat. Pink plumes. Yellowish tie.

We know that there were then alongside hussars, dragoons, and *chasseurs*, regiments of *cavalry* proper. It was, minus the breastplate and helmet, what we later called the big cavalry.

VI

7

Artillery Officers

One of these two officers seems to belong to the light artillery;
he wears the copper helmet of the *dragon* adorned with a red plume,
which must have been an exception; the other retained the horned
hat in use in the foot artillery. Their uniforms are completely blue
with red piping. Red *soutaches* adorn the pants and the waistcoat. Sabre grips take various shapes, boots are strong and light. What does
not vary is the type of the figures, which are shaved and adorned only
with small, very short whiskers.

VII

8

Chasseur à Cheval

Black helmet with short mane seeming to fall in front and behind. Green tights coat and pants with red piping; red, white and blue braids are arranged on the shoe to form a tricolour point.

A more complete description of the armament and uniform of this cavalry can be found in the *Uniforms* supplement.

VIII

9

Volunteer of the 1ᵉʳ Bataillon de Paris

Black helmet with a straight half-mane and copper ornaments; he is surrounded by a tiger band, blue coat, with white lapels and rolled up. White breeches, black gaiters, green epaulettes.

Also see our *Uniforms* supplement for details about Volunteer National Guardsmen.

IX

10

Dragoon and Hussard

The dragoon conforms to the type described in our supplement. His helmet is without visor; a thick mane further enhances the energetic character of a profile endowed with long moustaches.

His companion the *hussard* offers us the profile of this astonishing hairstyle that we have already seen plate 3. The red plume has lost none of its dimensions: it is casually surrounded by a brown flame with red piping. Dolman and green pants; red collar and *soutaches*. The gloves are yellow; the scabbard of the sabre is leather trimmed with copper.

11

Hussar (Same provenance)

The republican *hussards* that we usually represent are in conformity
with the type of our plates 3 and 10. This one proves that there was
another one wearing not the dolman with braids, but a green coat
with lapels and sides, long, pink collar and facings. Green pants and
waistcoat; the pants are protected by a fawn sheepskin whose edges are
jagged Greek style. He buttoned on the side according to the model
which was baptised with the name of *chutmari*. The band is red.

The hairstyle remains the same: braids of hair falling on the front
to frame the face, shako surrounded by a black flame with a red thread
fixed by a white cord; red plume. Where does the underfoot that at-
taches the unbuttoned pants to this shoe with a spur come from? . . .
Mystery!

XI

12

Mounted Grenadier

His uniform, weaponry and equipment meet the very full description given in our supplement. Brown fur hat with white plate, red plume and cord. Blue flap with red cuff and collar, rolled up and basques, white waistcoat and panties. Black boots, buffalo-cuffed gloves. Blue saddle cloth trimmed with yellow.

XII

13

Drum

The buffalo harness floats all slumped: the child has unhooked his big drum held on the shoulder with the help of a strap which should join the circle of the box. This load is not easy, his body tosses around in his blue coat which is too large; his hat with the red pompom is flattened like a harlequin hat. The nankeen pants show bare ankles, the shoes have become slippers, but that does not prevent the kid from walking proudly with long strides.

Plate 20 shows that almost all of our drums were children then.

And when you think that a minister of war cut our drums in half before 1870 so as not to inconvenience grown men!

XIII

14

Infantryman and Sous-Officier

The calm demeanour and almost regular demeanour of the non-commissioned officer contrast with the dismal pose of the soldier. The tie hangs down; the sleeves of his green coat are torn; he only has a brown stocking left, the hem of his nankeen pants threatens to ruin. A spoon and a fork with two points, crossed behind its cockade on each side of the pompom, complete its air of marauding soldier. A handkerchief tight to the biceps appears to protect an injury.

See similar to our numbers 10 and 17.

15

Chasseurs à Pied

These *chasseurs* differ a bit from the type described in our supplement. One, who looks like a corporal, wears the volunteer helmet. His short coat is black with blue facings. Bluish pants with dark blue stripes. Yellow tie. Red epaulettes. White trims on the sleeve.

His neighbour has a completely black uniform, with a light blue collar and turn-up. His hat is placed backwards. Red epaulets and plumes; yellowish upholstery. The shoes were transformed into slippers held in place by cords crossed above the ankle of the foot which is one as always.

XV

16

Grenadier of the Line

Black fur hat with copper plate. White coat, jacket and breeches. The lapels, the collar and the facings are red, the gaiters black. He is not wearing a haversack, but we see a sort of satchel hanging next to his pouch.

It is a last sample of the old army which will take the blue coat when the enlistment will merge the regiments and battalions of vol-unteers.

XVI

17

The helmeted volunteer feels his suburb from a league. A friend of a certain luxury, he has rolled up his sleeve to show a piece of cuff, he exhibits a pocket handkerchief elegantly tied to his dress and an adornment charm descends on his left thigh. The pretty knot of his big tie, the spoon that shows its head on the back of the coat and the bread impaled in his bayonet are all characteristic details. One of his shoes is held in place by a buckle. The other is tied with a string. Zebra on one side, squared on the other, like those breeches, partly from the Middle Ages. The white pants with blue stripes are too short not to have belonged to some brother in arms.

We have described the neighbour's gourmet assortment in the supplement: his blue police cap with a red turban is to be seen as a sample of the primitive model.

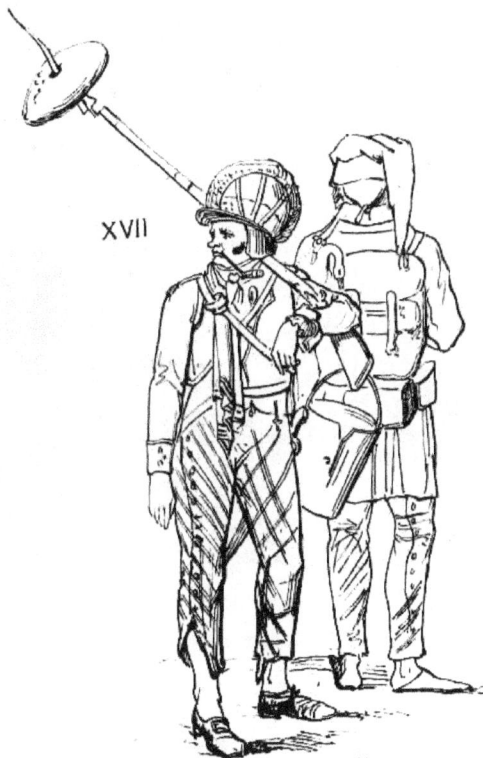

XVII

18

Cuirassiers

Zix is an artist from Strasbourg who was able to study the soldiers of the Army of the Rhine and Moselle from nature.

Not content with a supplement of picturesque illustrations for the geographical part of the *Journal de Fricasse* , my friend Charles Mehle kindly put Zix's engraving at my disposal. But their size made reproduction difficult. I had to content myself with detaching a group of two *cuirassiers* seated on the threshold of an Alsatian house.

We know that the *cuirassiers* formed the 8th Cavalry regiment in 1799. Hence their resemblance to the riders of the other plate 6.

XVIII

19

Camp Huts

These huts or shelters, which are mentioned in our journal, were made of branches. We see that they affect three shapes: an oblong shape, no doubt intended for soldiers; a pyramidal shape, less spacious, intended for non-commissioned officers; a conical shape, whose more complete fence announces a camp of officers.

The sentry watching at the door leaves no doubt about this last point. He is currently blowing a call horn, which gives him the dual functions of sentry and guard trumpet.

XIX

Infantry Gathering

Real representation of a parade of the French guard in Mannheim in October 1795.

This plate is excessively hostile. We shouldn't take our title literally. The German designer, whom I also hold to be sincere, took the moment not of the parade itself, but of the gathering that precedes it.

Housed with the townspeople, the soldiers gradually arrived and moved to the front of the line indicated by the three officers who had just put the sabre in their hands.

In this troop appear, according to custom, detachments of all the passing corps in the place and certainly also isolated soldiers, crippled, used for the service. From there, a strongly variegated look that the artist will have exaggerated further to offer models of each kind.

The four small drums which are in the hand on the far right would suffice to show that the command has not yet been heard. These are children whose oldest has not reached twelfth year. Behind them, the drum major charms his waiting with a few fancy reels.

The officers, seen on the back, have an ample grey or brown coat, on which stands only the gorget, insignia of the command.

The soldiers all seem to belong to either the volunteer battalions or the rural legions referred to in our supplement. We notice, in fact, in the second line, fur-lined hats, peasant hats; we can see one of the pikes which still figured in the armament of these non-combatants. One of them, a primitive sapper, holds the axe on his shoulder and the pipe in his mouth. His neighbour wears Turkish pants, and seems to want to conceal the disasters of his uniform under a white blanket. They could not hide their tattered outfits in this way. Many of the shoes are damaged; a young soldier has completely bare feet.

On the other hand, what is nowhere missing is the spoon: everyone wears this precious utensil in their buttonhole, hat or bonnet. A few cans and pots can also be seen here and there; the loaves are perforated for the passage of a cord which retains them at the side, unless they are not passed with the bayonet. A quarter of meat is even thus exhibited next to the spade carrier. It should be noted that there is not here a single one of the plumes which abound in our previous plates. But we are in 1795 and the French who have just entered Mannheim have made a very tough campaign. Their blue clothes are not only worn out by victory, they are especially ripped and torn by the steps and bivouacs on winter nights. From there this strange glance, which still exceeds, it is necessary of the to admit, all that one could suppose of the aspect of the republican troops. But the poverty of their appearance can only further increase the memory of their courage and their patriotism.

LEONAUR

ALSO FROM LEONAUR
AVAILABLE IN SOFTCOVER OR HARDCOVER WITH DUST JACKET

THE FALL OF THE MOGHUL EMPIRE OF HINDUSTAN *by H. G. Keene*—By the beginning of the nineteenth century, as British and Indian armies under Lake and Wellesley dominated the scene, a little over half a century of conflict brought the Moghul Empire to its knees.

LADY SALE'S AFGHANISTAN *by Florentia Sale*—An Indomitable Victorian Lady's Account of the Retreat from Kabul During the First Afghan War.

THE CAMPAIGN OF MAGENTA AND SOLFERINO 1859 *by Harold Carmichael Wylly*—The Decisive Conflict for the Unification of Italy.

FRENCH'S CAVALRY CAMPAIGN *by J. G. Maydon*—A Special Correspondent's View of British Army Mounted Troops During the Boer War.

CAVALRY AT WATERLOO *by Sir Evelyn Wood*—British Mounted Troops During the Campaign of 1815.

THE SUBALTERN *by George Robert Gleig*—The Experiences of an Officer of the 85th Light Infantry During the Peninsular War.

NAPOLEON AT BAY, 1814 *by F. Loraine Petre*—The Campaigns to the Fall of the First Empire.

NAPOLEON AND THE CAMPAIGN OF 1806 *by Colonel Vachée*—The Napoleonic Method of Organisation and Command to the Battles of Jena & Auerstädt.

THE COMPLETE ADVENTURES IN THE CONNAUGHT RANGERS *by William Grattan*—The 88th Regiment during the Napoleonic Wars by a Serving Officer.

BUGLER AND OFFICER OF THE RIFLES *by William Green & Harry Smith*—With the 95th (Rifles) during the Peninsular & Waterloo Campaigns of the Napoleonic Wars.

NAPOLEONIC WAR STORIES *by Sir Arthur Quiller-Couch*—Tales of soldiers, spies, battles & sieges from the Peninsular & Waterloo campaigns.

CAPTAIN OF THE 95TH (RIFLES) *by Jonathan Leach*—An officer of Wellington's sharpshooters during the Peninsular, South of France and Waterloo campaigns of the Napoleonic wars.

RIFLEMAN COSTELLO *by Edward Costello*—The adventures of a soldier of the 95th (Rifles) in the Peninsular & Waterloo Campaigns of the Napoleonic wars.

LEONAUR

ALSO FROM LEONAUR
AVAILABLE IN SOFTCOVER OR HARDCOVER WITH DUST JACKET

THE 9TH—THE KING'S (LIVERPOOL REGIMENT) IN THE GREAT WAR 1914 - 1918 *by Enos H. G. Roberts*—Mersey to mud—war and Liverpool men.

THE GAMBARDIER *by Mark Severn*—The experiences of a battery of Heavy artillery on the Western Front during the First World War.

FROM MESSINES TO THIRD YPRES *by Thomas Floyd*—A personal account of the First World War on the Western front by a 2/5th Lancashire Fusilier.

THE IRISH GUARDS IN THE GREAT WAR - VOLUME 1 *by Rudyard Kipling*—Edited and Compiled from Their Diaries and Papers—The First Battalion.

THE IRISH GUARDS IN THE GREAT WAR - VOLUME 1 *by Rudyard Kipling*—Edited and Compiled from Their Diaries and Papers—The Second Battalion.

ARMOURED CARS IN EDEN *by K. Roosevelt*—An American President's son serving in Rolls Royce armoured cars with the British in Mesopatamia & with the American Artillery in France during the First World War.

CHASSEUR OF 1914 *by Marcel Dupont*—Experiences of the twilight of the French Light Cavalry by a young officer during the early battles of the great war in Europe.

TROOP HORSE & TRENCH *by R.A. Lloyd*—The experiences of a British Lifeguardsman of the household cavalry fighting on the western front during the First World War 1914-18.

THE EAST AFRICAN MOUNTED RIFLES *by C.J. Wilson*—Experiences of the campaign in the East African bush during the First World War.

THE LONG PATROL *by George Berrie*—A Novel of Light Horsemen from Gallipoli to the Palestine campaign of the First World War.

THE FIGHTING CAMELIERS *by Frank Reid*—The exploits of the Imperial Camel Corps in the desert and Palestine campaigns of the First World War.

STEEL CHARIOTS IN THE DESERT *by S. C. Rolls*—The first world war experiences of a Rolls Royce armoured car driver with the Duke of Westminster in Libya and in Arabia with T.E. Lawrence.

WITH THE IMPERIAL CAMEL CORPS IN THE GREAT WAR *by Geoffrey Inchbald*—The story of a serving officer with the British 2nd battalion against the Senussi and during the Palestine campaign.

www.ingramcontent.com/pod-product-compliance
Lightning Source LLC
Chambersburg PA
CBHW021109090426
42738CB00006B/564